A SLICE THROUGH THE WORLD

CONTEMPORARY ARTISTS' DRAWINGS

Drawing Room is the place to discover
contemporary drawing and is internationally
renowned for stimulating debate around
the nature and purpose of drawing today.
Through free exhibitions, artists' talks, practical
workshops and a unique library it nurtures
the production of drawings and promotes
understanding of them. It collaborates with
institutions to expand research, produce
publications and tour its exhibitions. Drawing
Room is a charity and is affiliated to the
professional studio organisation Tannery Arts.

Modern Art Oxford is one of the UK's most
exciting and influential contemporary art
spaces. Renowned for its bold, progressive and
international artistic programme, it plays a central
role in Oxford's cultural landscape. Shaped
by a longstanding commitment to education
and diversity, it encourages public engagement
with creativity and visual arts through world-
class exhibitions, artist commissions, events and
participatory activities. Modern Art Oxford is
a charity, and is free and open to all.

A SLICE THROUGH THE WORLD
CONTEMPORARY ARTISTS' DRAWINGS

RUBY ONYINYECHI AMANZE   MILANO CHOW   NIDHAL CHAMEKH
KATE DAVIS   KARL HAENDEL   DAVID HAINES   IAN KIAER
CIPRIAN MUREȘAN   DAVID MUSGRAVE   WURA-NATASHA OGUNJI
KATHY PRENDERGAST   MASSINISSA SELMANI   LUCY SKAER
BARBARA WALKER

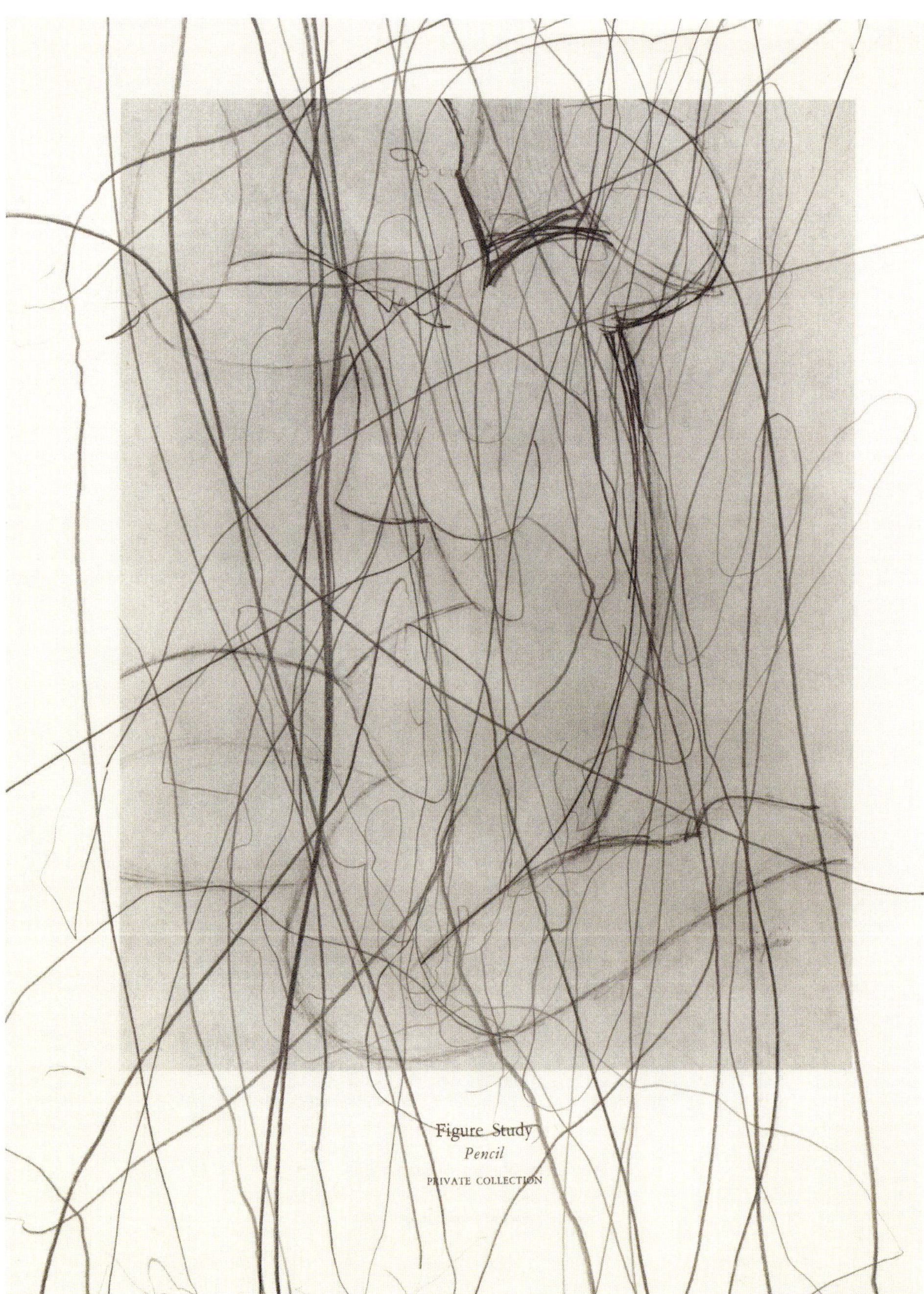

Kate Davis

Disgrace III, 2009

Pencil on page from monograph, 44 × 35 cm

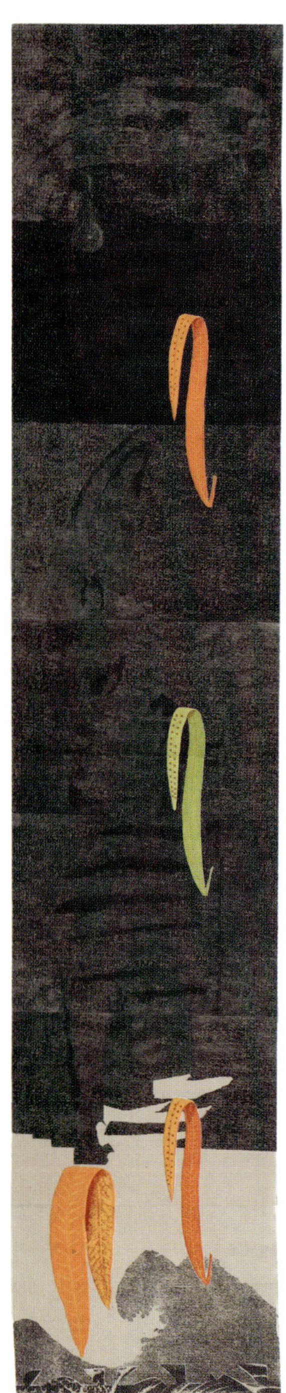 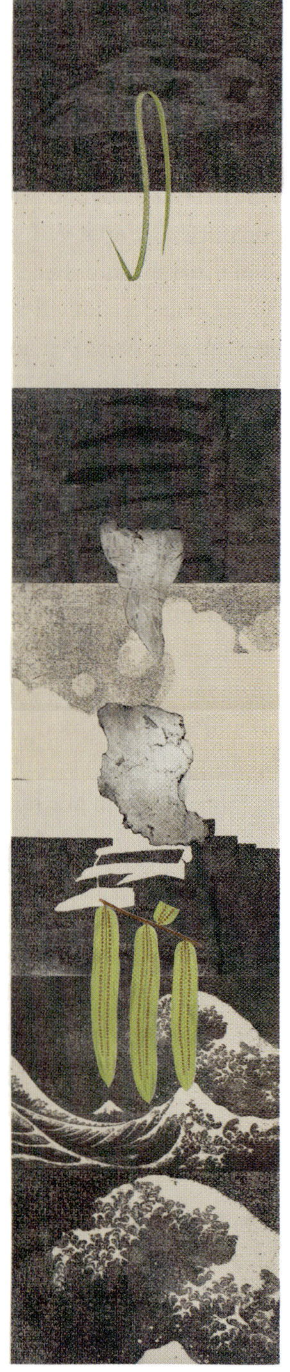

Lucy Skaer
Available Fonts, 2017 (detail)
Chine-collé of etching, wood engraving and found material on paper,
142 × 28 cm; 142 × 28 cm; 162 × 28 cm; 162 × 28 cm

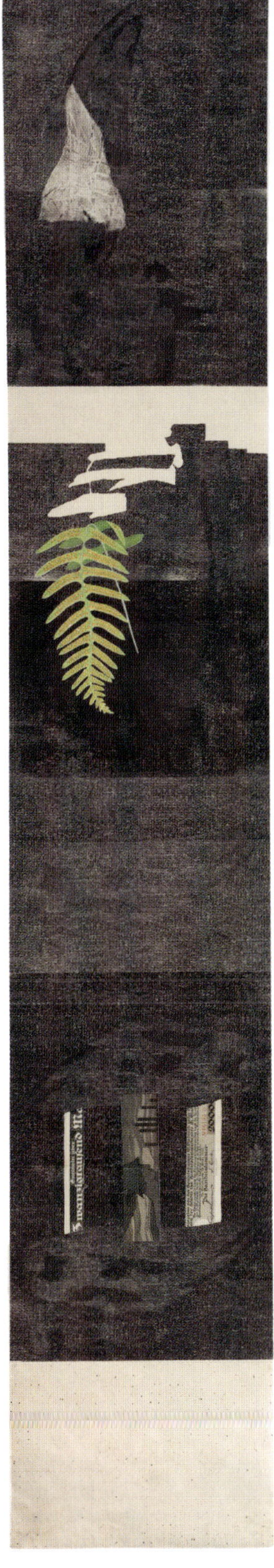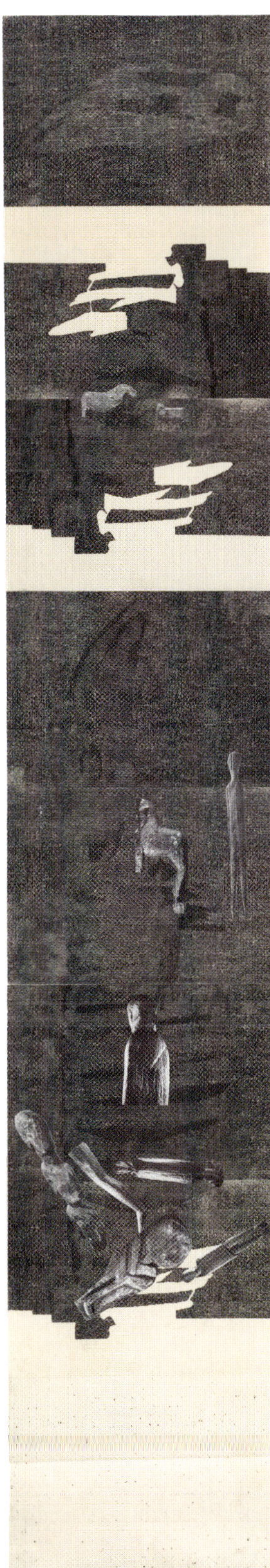

FOREWORD

Modern Art Oxford and Drawing Room are proud to jointly present *A Slice through the World: Contemporary Artists' Drawings*, a group exhibition that celebrates the sustained power of drawing in our digital age. Employing the traditional tools of drawing such as graphite and ink on paper, the featured artists react to contemporary conditions, as well as the histories – social, economic, environmental and cultural – that have shaped today's global politics. Across our two institutions in Oxford and London, we have assembled an expansive range of artworks by contemporary international artists who use drawing as a trans-historical technology of recording and response. Their works pay close attention to drawing's relationship to the complexities and problems of the past. What can drawn images tell us about our negotiation of history in this present moment? How might they offer paths towards future models of recognition, commemoration and action?

A Slice through the World presents an exciting variety of contemporary drawings from the last decade, alongside a selection of newly produced works, by artists from 10 different countries whose practices variously comment on post-internet culture and new technologies, literary and cultural histories, environmental concerns, and image circulation. Together, these artists signal the resilience of drawing as a means of exploring and responding to contemporary questions of dialogue and representation.

The exhibition pays homage to the major group show *[Drawing]*, staged in 1972 at what was then known as the Museum of Modern Art Oxford. It was organised under the directorship of Peter Ibsen and proposed by artists John Murphy and Peter Waldron, featuring an impressive roster of over 40 artists. *[Drawing]* put forward a case for the medium's significance within an era often remembered for the withdrawal of both artistic skill and the physical art object, and committed to an international perspective on the avant-garde, at a time when this remained unusual in the UK's contemporary art scene.

The present exhibition showcases an attention to skill and detail, by looking at one of the oldest technologies (drawing) as it meets the newest forms of digitised image culture. While the artistic practices of 1972 heralded a move away from the physical artwork and towards conceptual, installation and performance art, today, despite rapid developments in technology, many artists are recommitting to the materiality of paper and pencil. What accounts for this endurance of drawing? The two essays in this publication consider that skill, the investment of time, and the tangible materiality of drawing are a means to slow things down in an age of social media and digital exhaustion. The ambitious scale of works, despite the modesty of drawing's means, is also scrutinised. The technological and mass media excess of contemporary life has, it seems, instigated a revival of drawing, particularly its ability to make and remake image culture, producing a scenario in which drawing can be framed not only as a medium, but as a multimedia strategy.

This exhibition tells us much about contemporary culture and our relationship to images, by arguing that the agency of drawing is amplified by the speed and hyper-accessibility of images in our digital lives. Drawing asks us to think about how we look at the world, and how we absorb information (often on an unconscious basis). By taking stock of how we understand (or fail to understand) the processes of looking, we might reflect on how looking and recording have changed in this new moment of technology. As artist Milano Chow explains: 'I learned to believe in the drawing technique as a thinking process.'

The exhibition's title, *A Slice through the World*, is inspired by 'Painting and the Graphic Arts,' a short essay written in 1917 by the German philosopher, theorist and cultural critic Walter Benjamin. He argued for drawing's fundamentally different orientation to the world (horizontal rather than vertical). Benjamin suggested that some drawings present cross sections of the world, and are symbolic of things in the world, i.e. signs, in distinction to painting 'containing the world.' Co-curator Stephanie Straine examines the legacy of these ideas in 'Nomadic Drawing,' an essay that contemplates the intermedial and migratory potential of drawing in the work of ruby onyinyechi amanze, Nidhal Chamekh,

Milano Chow, Ian Kiaer, Wura-Natasha Ogunji and Kathy Prendergast. Her co-curator Kate Macfarlane writes here on 'Drawing as Thinking through Material Encounter,' a humanist conception of drawing as connecting subjectivities through an exploration of works by Nidhal Chamekh, Kate Davis, Karl Haendel, David Haines, David Musgrave, Massinissa Selmani, Lucy Skaer and Barbara Walker.

This two-venue collaborative exhibition brings together a dynamic group of recent drawings by 14 British and international artists: ruby onyinyechi amanze, Milano Chow, Nidhal Chamekh, Kate Davis, Karl Haendel, David Haines, Ian Kiaer, Ciprian Mureşan, David Musgrave, Wura-Natasha Ogunji, Kathy Prendergast, Massinissa Selmani, Lucy Skaer and Barbara Walker. We are deeply indebted to the artists for their generously-spirited collaboration and dialogue during preparations for this exhibition.

Paul Hobson, Director
Emma Ridgway, Head of Programme
Modern Art Oxford

Mary Doyle and Kate Macfarlane
Co-Directors, Drawing Room

DRAW, V.T.I. PROTRACT, STRETCH, ELONGATE, TRACE,
(FURROW, FIGURE, LINE); DELINEATE, MAKE (PICTURE),
REPRESENT (OBJECT), BY DRAWING LINES, (ABS.) USE
PENCIL THUS; DESCRIBE IN WORDS; PRACTICE DELINEATION;
FRAME (DOCUMENT) IN DUE FORM, COMPOSE; FORMULATE;
WRITE OUT.

DRAWING, N. IN VBL. SENSES; ESP. : ART OF REPRESENTING
BY LINE, DELINEATION WITHOUT COLOUR OR WITH SINGLE
COLOUR ; PRODUCT OF THIS, BLACK AND WHITE OR
MONOCHROME SKETCH.

DEFINITIONS FROM THE CONCISE
OXFORD DICTIONARY.

THE FORM OF THIS EXHIBITION HAS ~~GROWN~~ DEVELOPED
FORTUITOUSLY FROM AN INTEREST IN 'DRAWING',
AS OPPOSED TO DRAWING AS PSEUDO-PAINTING, OR
A PRELIMINARY STAGE TOWARDS PAINTING OR
SCULPTURE ETC. IT WILL I HOPE HELP TO SHOW
THE CENTRAL FUNCTION OF DRAWING AS A
VEHICLE FOR IDEA - VISUAL INFORMATION.

JOHN MURPHY

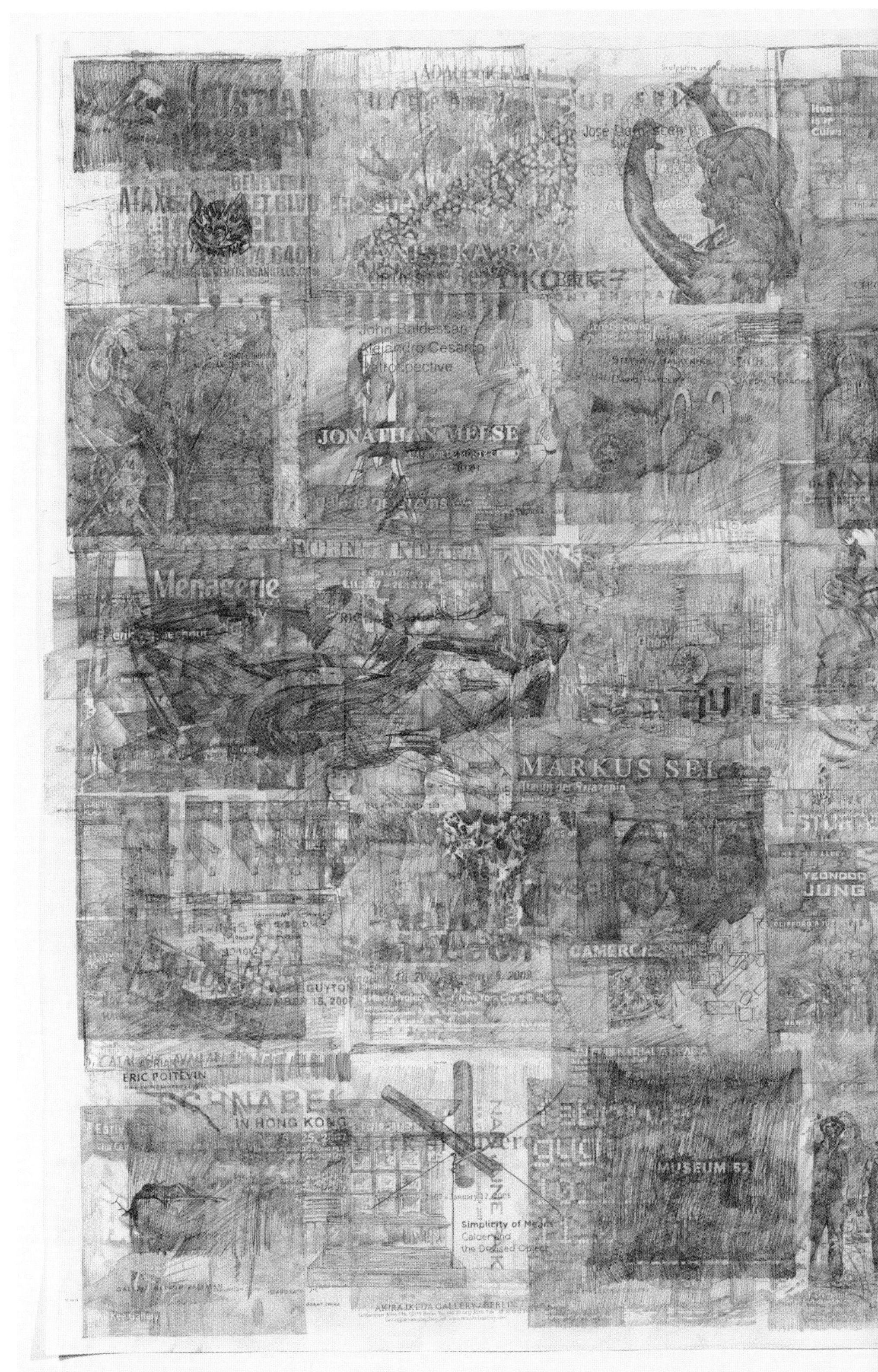

NOMADIC DRAWING

The exhibition *A Slice through the World* recognises and returns to a significant moment in Modern Art Oxford's institutional history: the major group exhibition *[Drawing]*, staged in 1972 at what was then known as the Museum of Modern Art Oxford.[1] It brought together recent drawings by over 40 artists, operating as a selective survey of contemporary art in that moment, or what one local reviewer described as 'a mini-survey of the avant-garde.'[2] British and international artists included Robert Barry, Mel Bochner, Hanne Darboven, Rita Donagh, Barry Flanagan, Dan Graham, Derek Jarman, Bob Law, Agnes Martin, Robert Smithson, Edda Renouf, Richard Tuttle, Lawrence Weiner, and Richard Wentworth. The majority of artists in the show did not work exclusively with drawing, but the exhibition demonstrated what it offered, as a medium or methodology, to their wider practice (a notion perhaps equally true of the present exhibition). The selection was comprised mostly of small-scale works on paper (enabling a global roster of artists to be presented without prohibitive transportation costs), with some excursions into painting, photography, audio and text-based work, and a couple of site-specific wall drawings.

Curated under the directorship of Peter Ibsen, two British artists, John Murphy and Peter Waldron, 'initially suggested the show and helped considerably in its organisation.'[3] Presented at the very height of conceptual art's power and visibility in Europe and North America, with its ideas-led prioritising of text over image, the front cover of *[Drawing]*'s modest exhibition catalogue offered a close-up of a dictionary page featuring various definitions of drawing (p.16). The exhibition's one-word title was overlaid across the text, and neatly framed in square brackets, as if to demarcate a particular space, or role, for drawing at this time. As an overview of many of the practitioners associated with minimal, conceptual, process and land art, *[Drawing]* put forward a case for the centrality of drawing within an era often characterised by the departure of both artistic skill and the physical art object (the oft-entangled ideas of deskilling and dematerialisation).[4]

While there are certainly many notable differences between these two exhibitions of 1972 and 2018 respectively, it is intriguing to observe what is shared by the two artistic cohorts (separated by more than 45 years), in particular their continued commitment to drawing, despite conditions seemingly unfavourable to the medium: be that the erasure of the artist's hand favoured by early 1970s conceptual art, or the proliferation of digital imaging technologies today. The private view invitation declared that *[Drawing]* was 'an exhibition of work in which drawing is more of an end than a means to another medium.'[5] As an echo of this 1972 position, the present exhibition is equally unconcerned with the categories of preliminary or working drawings. The drawings gathered together in *A Slice through the World* absolutely cannot be assigned the status of preparatory studies or

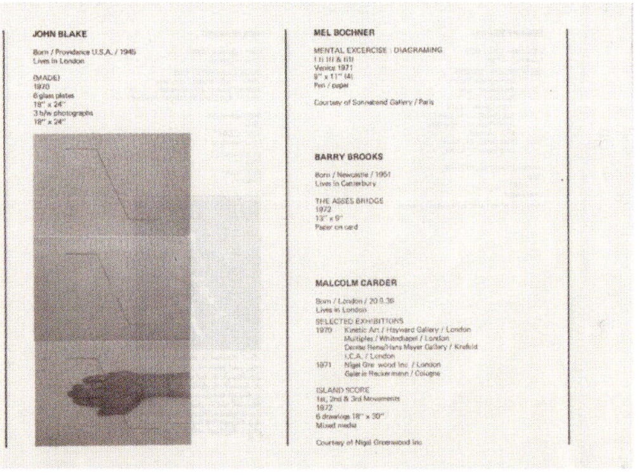

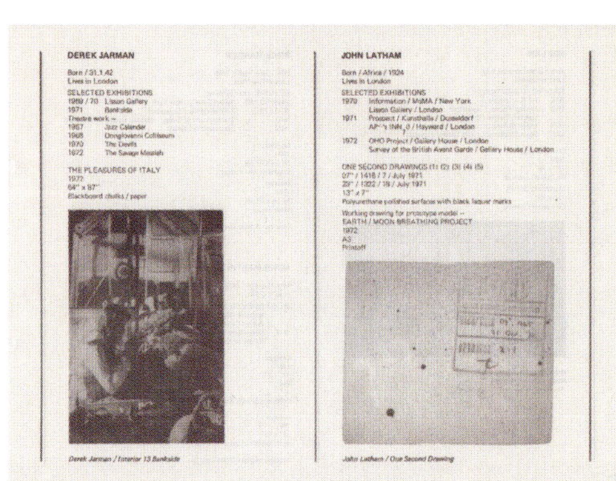

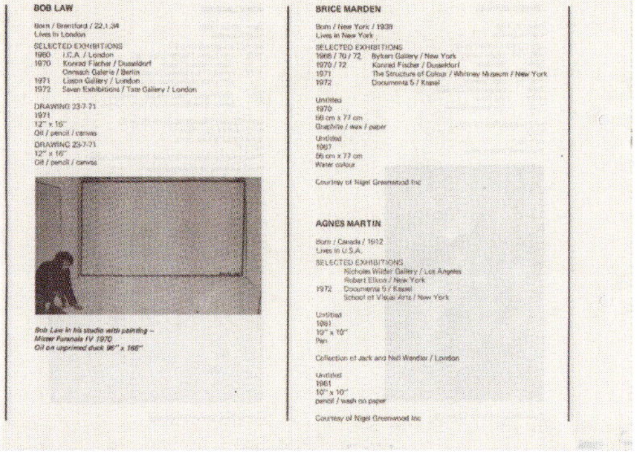

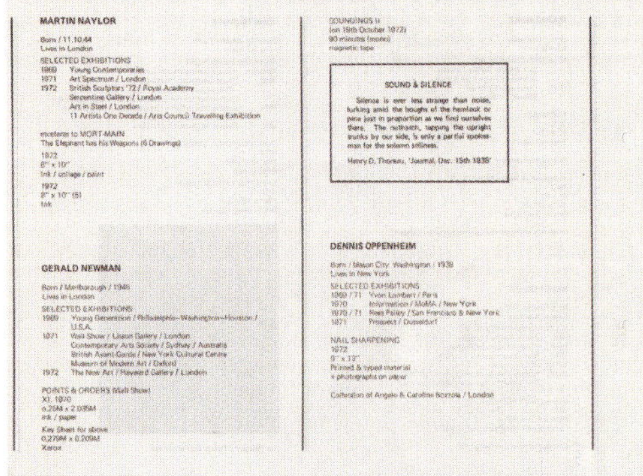

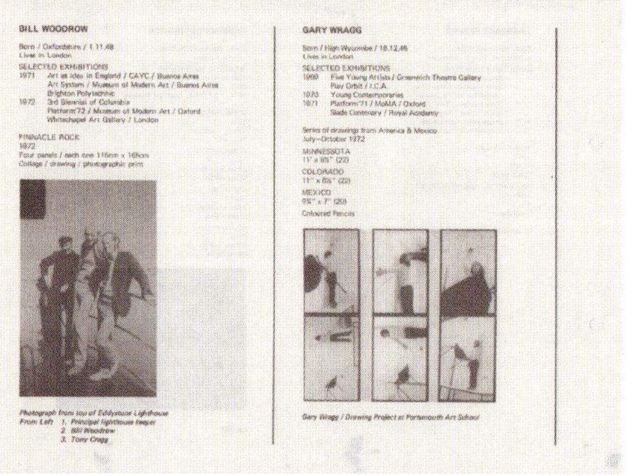

Cover and pages from *[Drawing]* exhibition catalogue, 1972,
the Museum of Modern Art Oxford, *[Drawing]* exhibition folder,
Modern Art Oxford archive

quickly executed sketches (to follow traditional medium hierarchies and the long-held notion of drawing's 'primacy'). What drawing is doing for artists today is far more radical, complex and expansive, with the potential to provoke major innovations within practice – a fact that has always been true, throughout its long history as a medium. These are all autonomous, highly finished works, 'ends rather than means,' often reached after the production of allied work in other mediums like film, performance, or photography. Art historian Lucy Steeds has suggested that: '… the significance today of *[Drawing]* in Oxford lies in its confounding claims to medium specificity – with the square brackets of the show's very title suggesting the quasi-incidental relevance of drawing being the medium of choice for the work presented.'[6]

[Drawing]'s insistence on plural temporalities, broad-based definitions and the potential 'ends' of drawing offered a partial – albeit 'confounding' – retreat from the path towards total dematerialisation favoured by some artists and critics of the time. By extension, this exhibition of 2018 might be understood as an emphatic statement of re-materialisation in the face of the virtual. Like the 1972 exhibition, it presents an alternative perspective on the international avant-garde, as seen through the lens of drawing. The works on view support the claim that making use of seemingly conservative or traditional materials can actually produce artistic positions of radicality – be that through process, materiality, subjects or histories.

What are the implications when drawing is not treated as a preparatory, instructional or diagrammatic tool, but conversely a final manifestation of a larger conceptual project?[7] To ask this is to make a claim for the medium in all its slipperiness, acknowledging its necessarily fractured and contested state, and to investigate its interstitial gaps; the boundaries that make it still so potent, and still useful, as a terminology. Now that drawing has been expanded so thoroughly, what would it mean to think again about its resilience in the face of this expansion, to return to a 'conventional' grounding in paper-based practices and challenge the negative inferences of that very description? The expanded field of drawing is widely understood; can we now demand more of the specifics of drawing?[8] I am using the 'specifics' of drawing as a kind of shorthand for those theoretical and material aspects that are intrinsic to the work that drawing does.

This demand involves incorporating intermediality without negating the material specificities of drawing. By intermediality I mean, following media theorist Lars Ellström, the 'phenomenon whereby the properties of all media partly intersect.'[9] This research concept, most commonly used in performance, theatre and cultural studies, is an imported, and innately hybrid, term that places difference at the core of exchange and relationality. In this way, it reflects the core curatorial principles of this exhibition, which seeks to recognise the shifting place of drawing within contemporary artists' practice. The exhibition's artists explore both the material conditions of drawing as a medium, and its ever-changing capacity to assimilate and synthesise other artistic, media and research forms. As artist and drawing theorist Tania Kovats has stated: 'Drawing is a mechanism for exploration as much as a tool for representation.'[10]

My argument is that drawing's ability to migrate across boundaries (such as those maintained between the categories of representation and abstraction, or between the past and the present) remains implicit to this day. What I want to do is think about drawing's migration in terms of intermediality: the bleed between materials, or between moments in time and space (in that intersection Ellström identifies), and how artists thematise this using drawing. By fostering migration within a practice, for example by transgressing 'style' categories and medium boundaries, or embracing geographic migration and its effects on a practice, the artists featured in this exhibition insist on the resilience of drawing, which is by necessity material rather than immaterial. Wura-Natasha Ogunji, Kathy Prendergast, Ian Kiaer, ruby onyinyechi amanze, Nidhal Chamekh and Milano Chow all, in distinct ways, contemplate the intermedial and migratory potential of drawing.

The constitutionally intermedial relationships tracked throughout this take on contemporary drawing are always grounded by a conceptual interest in a basic materiality: paper, pencil, ink and other rudimentary tools associated with drawing in the most straightforward of terms. This is a concerted attempt to avoid gathering artists together merely along stylistic lines; to forge instead links based on conceptual affinity, processual and political strategies, and temporal elasticity. I argue for the importance of drawing as an innovating factor for these artists, particularly in its ability to operate on other aspects of artistic production.

'Paper as body'[11]

Several artists in this exhibition explore spatial manifestations of drawing, by which I mean graphic renderings that variously articulate the body's (and the subject's) relationship to the world – via maps, borders and boundary lines, explorations of the body-as-landscape, and architectural/archival splicings. There is a tension here between abstraction and figuration, and between the intimacy of bodily trace or pressure and the data distance of models and maps.

In Kathy Prendergast's work, drawing can be understood as an operation that questions the process of delineation in relation to territory, borders and settlements, with a consideration for how this delineation implicates language, identity and nationhood. Across her extensive body of work, there is a commitment to using secondary source materials, particularly maps and postcards. This use of pre-existing imagery, whether

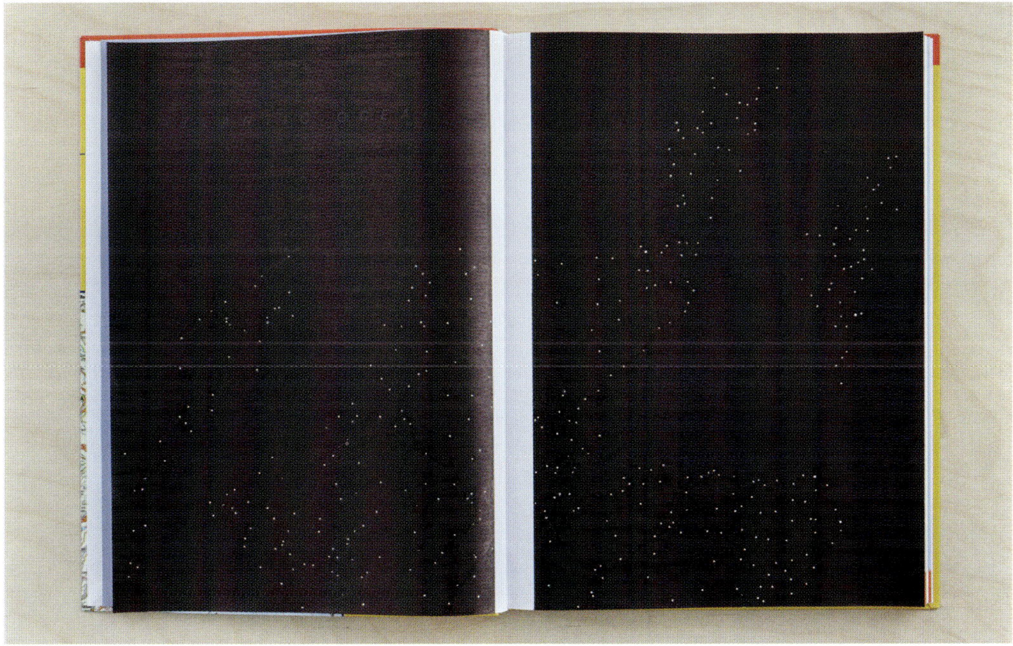

Kathy Prendergast
Atlas, 2016 (detail)
Set of 100 AA Road Atlas of Europe, ink, trestle tables,
30.5 × 43.5 × 1 cm (each atlas)

following spread
Kathy Prendergast
Atlas, 2016
Installation view

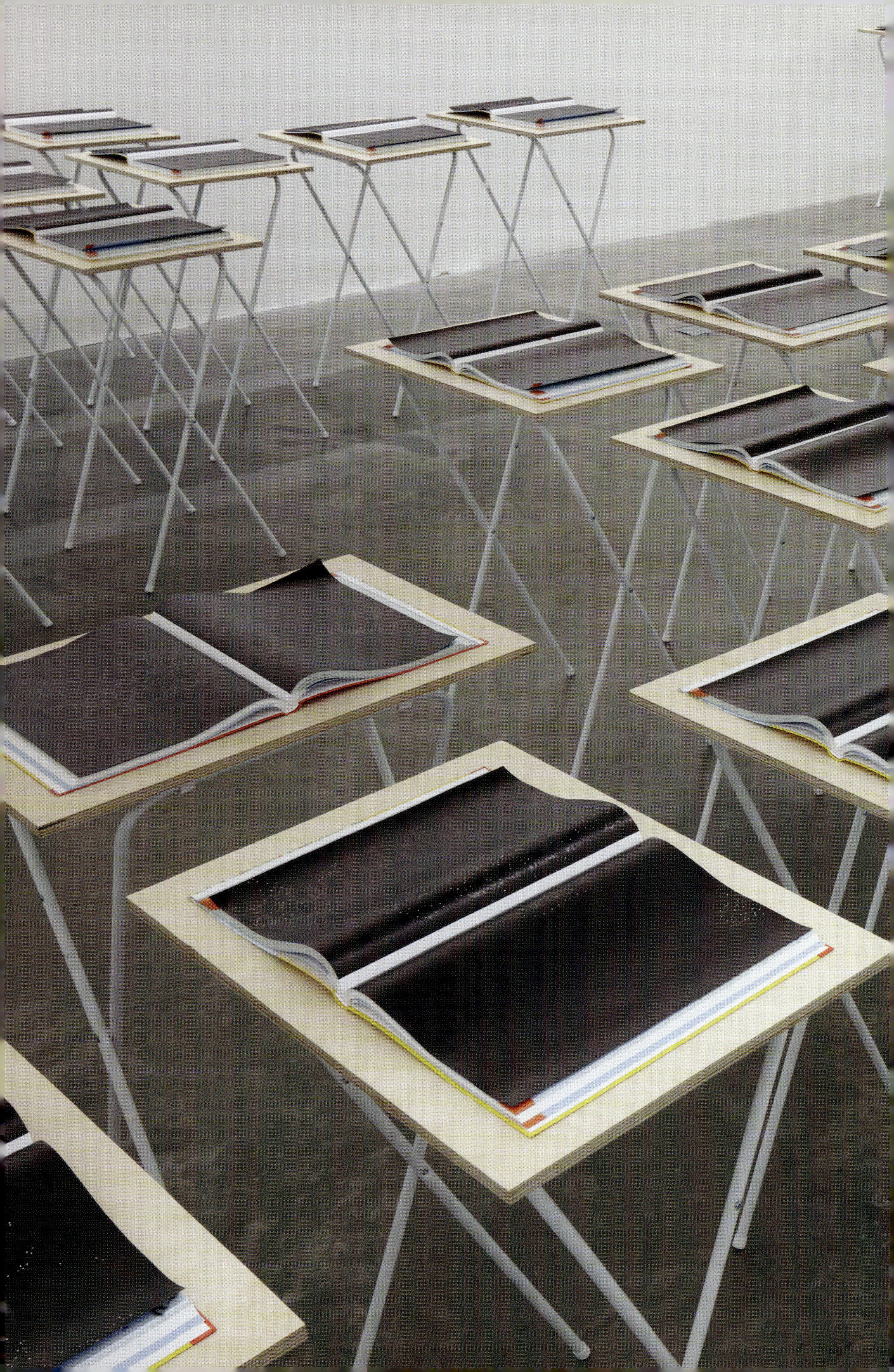

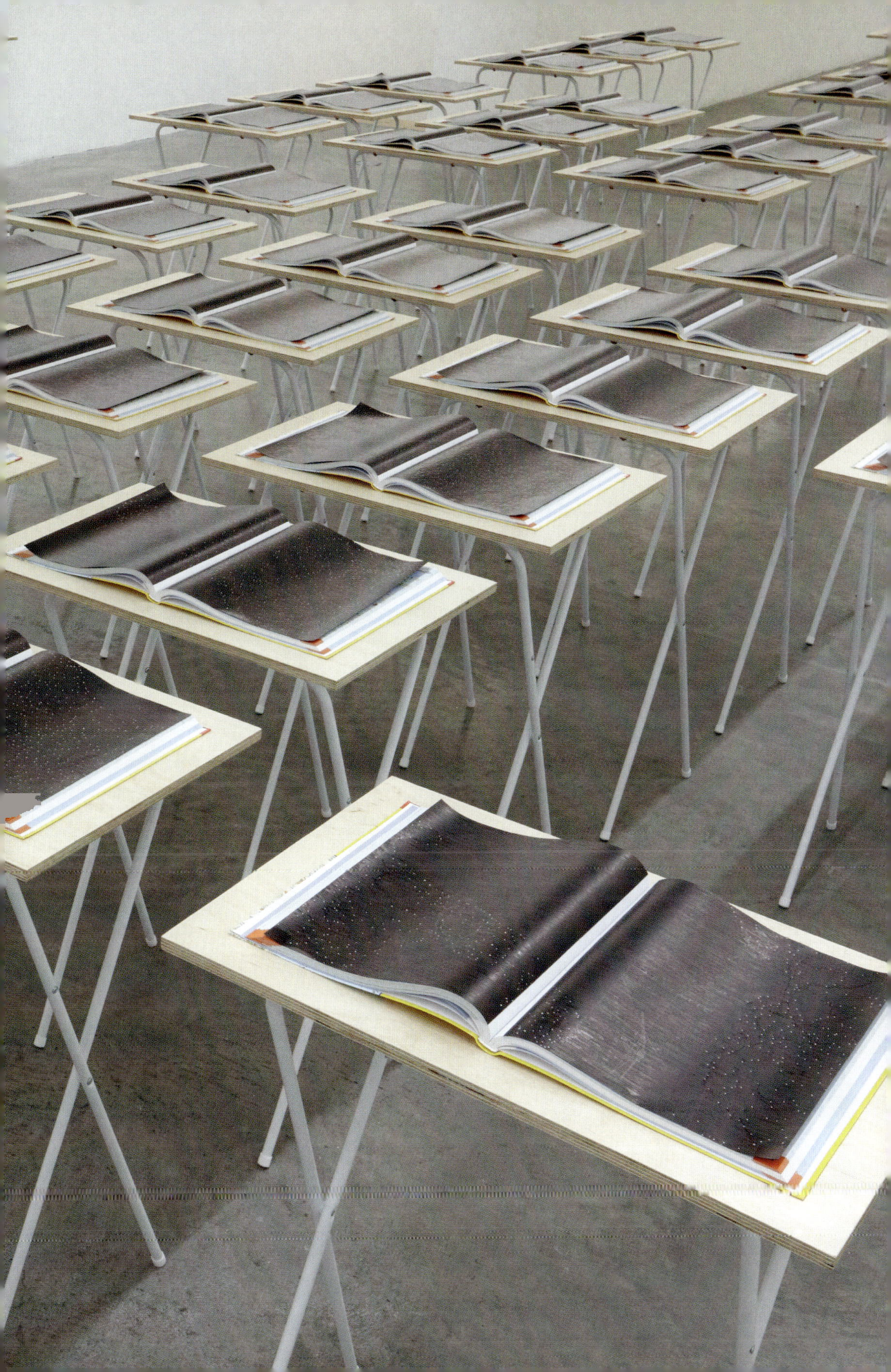

cartographic or photographic, is premised on
a deliberate act of distancing. Prendergast's
Atlas (2016, pp.19–21) is an installation of
100 copies of the AA Road Atlas of Europe
presented on individual trestle tables, arranged
in the gallery space so as to mimic the shape of
the European continent. Each atlas lies open at
a page that corresponds to its position within
the Europe created by the clusters of small tables,
around which visitors can walk. On the open
double-page spreads, Prendergast has used a
black ink pen to draw freehand horizontal lines
that collectively obscure all aspects of the map;
with the exception of the small white circles that
denote a city, town or village, which she carefully
draws around. By emphasising, not erasing, the
settlements and neglecting the borders, the
artist creates a version of Europe that captures
population spread and density, and deprioritises
delineation between neighbouring nations, and
between land and sea.

This is no simple act of geographic
obliteration, however. In these shimmering
black constellations of rectangular European
fragments, the horizontal bands of black ink
actually enable that which has been covered to
shine through, reflecting back from the inky
depths. The glossy paper provides a degree of
resistance to the action of erasure, revealing
the ghostly imprint of the cartographic
information underneath. As the artist notes, the
areas of the page that represent bodies of water
don't absorb the ink as well – the ink assumes
a more striated appearance, allowing you to

see the lines. In contrast, in the maps that show
only land, it's a denser feel, with the black ink
soaking in.[12] The map for Prendergast operates
in a manner akin to a photograph: it captures
a particular moment in time, fixing in print a
set of legal and diplomatic arrangements that
are, despite the veneer of permanence, subject
to potentially endless change and revision.

Atlas is a vital work that foregrounds the
horizontality of drawing practice within the
exhibition. It is the only work which retains
in display the horizontal alignment, which
is to say: the orientation of its making. In its
invitation for viewers to navigate the trestle
tables and approach the individual atlases as
both flat objects and planes of information,
Atlas emphasises the oblique orientation of
the viewers in relation to the artwork; the
many possibilities of the body in relation to
the level page. There is contained within this
horizontal slice equally the artist's body –
making, marking and looking over these open
pages – and the viewers' bodies, surveying
and encircling this continent-in-miniature. In
its ability to offer a slice through the world,
drawing here expresses its intermediality with
a simultaneously haptic and political pulse.

Wura-Natasha Ogunji's *The proof, an undersea
volcano, attraction, extraction, distraction* (2017,
pp.23–25) is a large-scale work across six
separate vertical panels, made using thread, ink
and graphite on a double layer of architectural
tracing paper. The tracing paper is delicate but

opposite page (detail) and following spread
Wura-Natasha Ogunji
The proof, an undersea volcano, attraction, extraction, distraction, 2017
Thread, graphite and ink on tracing paper, 152 × 366 cm

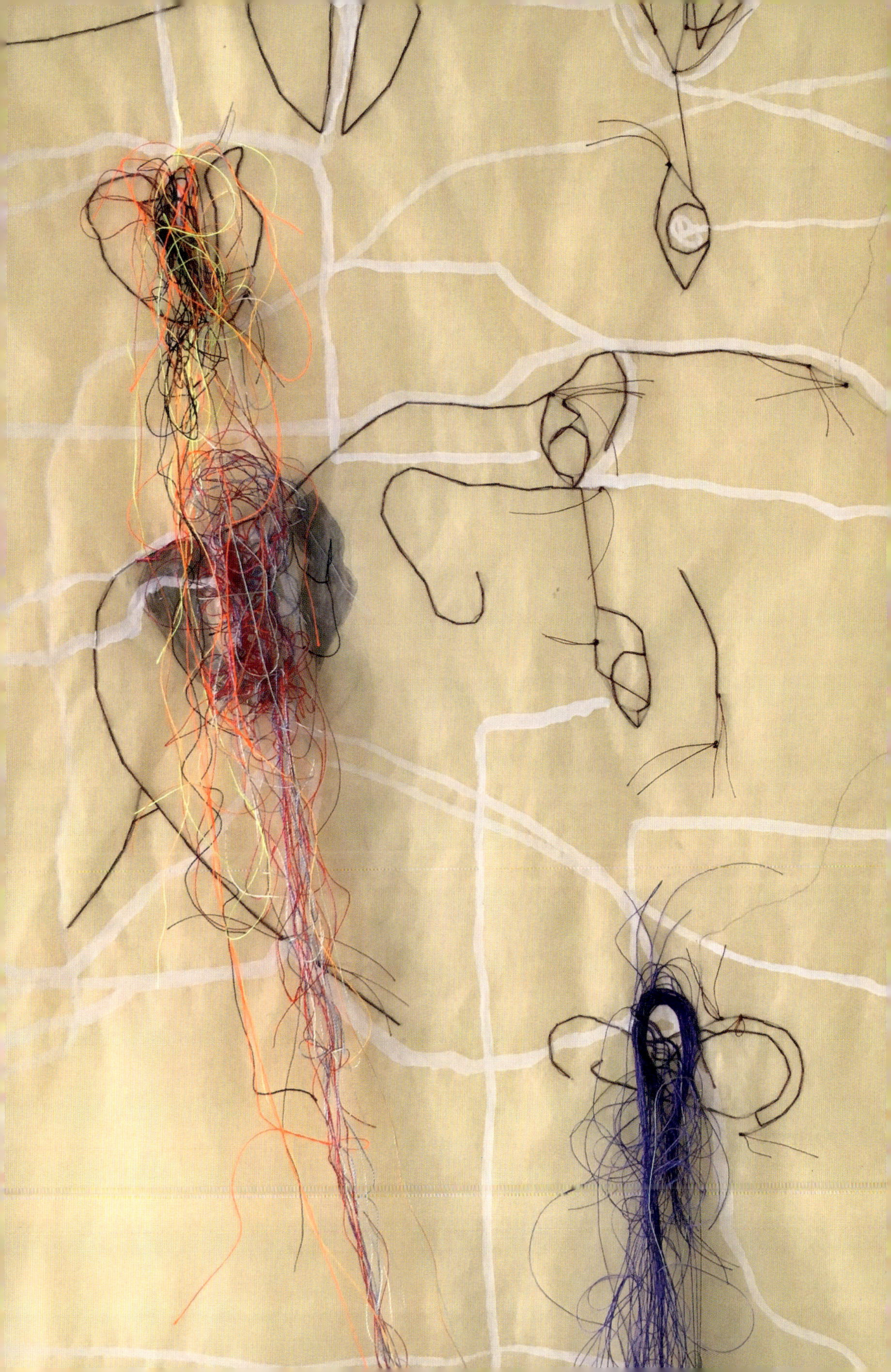

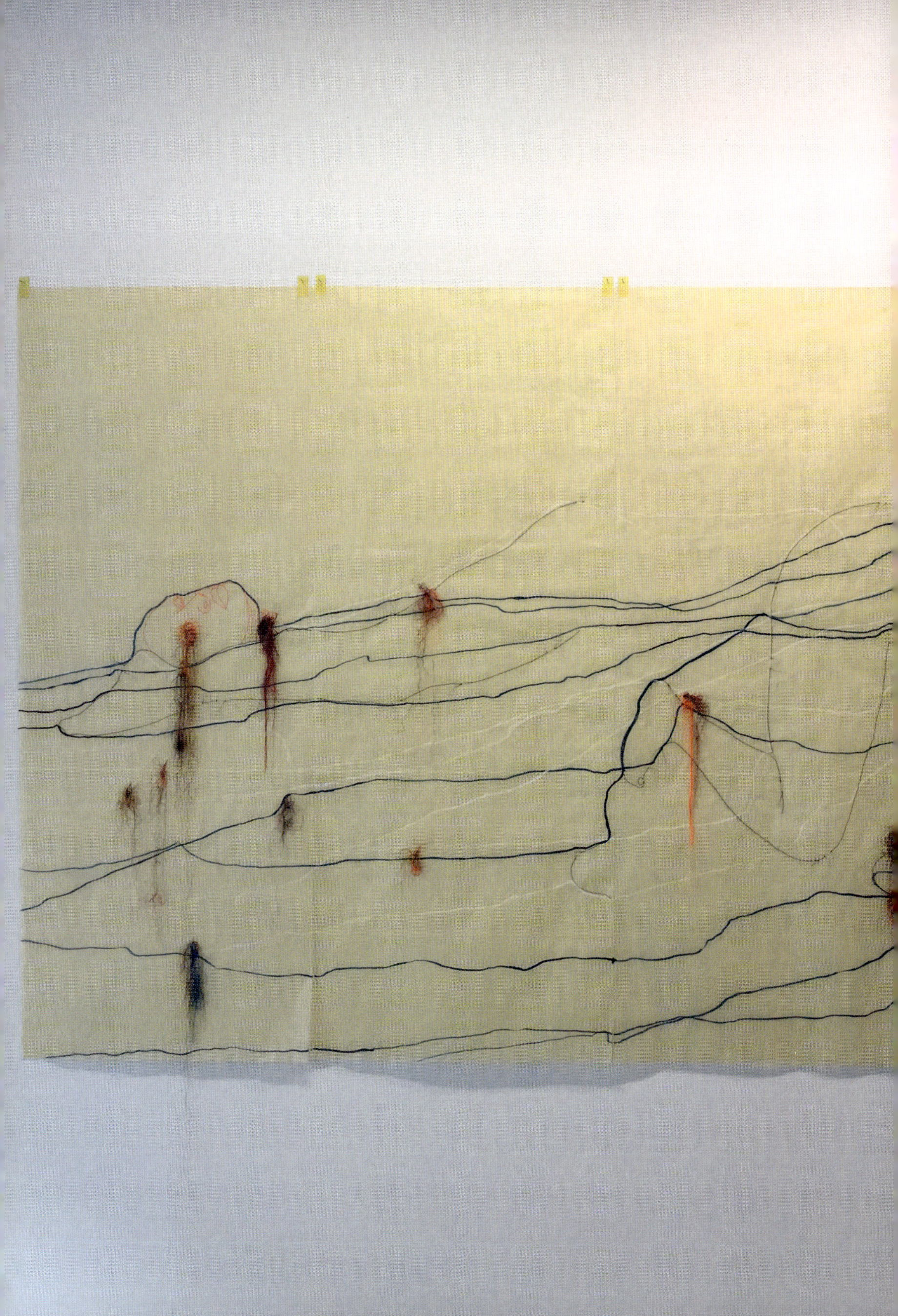

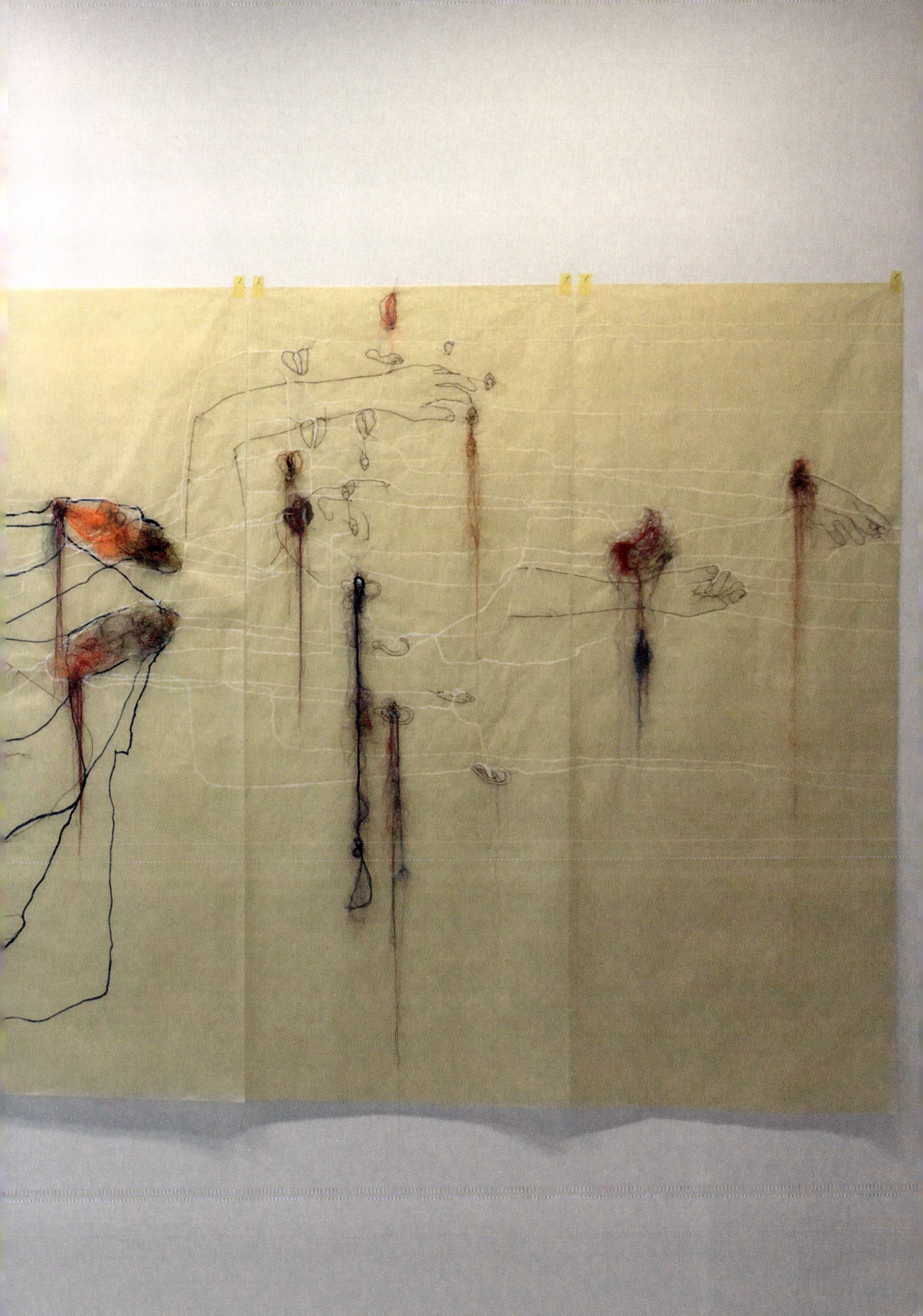

also surprisingly tough, resistant to a great deal of stitching and handling. Ogunji's drawing practice operates in the border zone between abstraction and figuration, and in this work we can understand the subject to be at once two female bodies, lying horizontally in space, and an abstract, sinuous land- or sea-scape. From the relentlessly intersecting ink lines, the conglomerations of fine, colourful threads, and the constant uncertainty of where body meets geography, there is provoked a sensation of contortion, of stretching the physical body and its spaces to a state beyond anatomical reality. The thread clusters that accumulate at eyes, mouths and wrists suggest the viscera of the body; a casual disregard for any internal/external partition. Embroidery or sewing for Ogunji is not a female-gendered activity.[13] In the work, the process of sewing is exclusively concerned with the action of drawing: the repetition and reiteration of the marks made through thread. Within the drawing's fifth panel, the body detaches components from itself and replicates these as part objects that proliferate across the surface of the tracing paper, particularly concentrated along a vertical axis above and below the face. Disembodied ears, mouths and noses form a cascade, interrupted or embellished in places by the gathering of thread clusters – in dark blues, purples, reds, and oranges.

The 'volcano' of the title is visualised through the entwined female bodies: their proneness is not relaxed, but rather suggests an erotic,

entangled tension that is about to erupt. Drawing for Ogunji is palpably haptic, but it is also very much about being alone, in the studio. It's a heady, private space for her, separate to the public space of her performance practice. Through her drawings she poses situations: what would happen if the body was suspended, twisted or contorted in space? She wants her drawings to evoke a sensual experience in the viewer. This poetic exploration of the body, particularly the visual repetition of its constituent parts, succeeds in collapsing the distance between landscape and flesh, between seemingly contradictory visual codes.[14]

There is a filmic quality to Ogunji's drawing practice, which is equally derived from the interrupted, film frame-like structure of the tracing paper panels (slicing the image into interstices) and the artist's method of projecting images onto or through the semi-transparent tracing paper, in part to assemble her montage of visual sources. Other artists in the exhibition share this interest in collapsing the technologies of drawing and film, such as Milano Chow and Ciprian Mureşan. Although they approach this intermediality from wildly differing perspectives, together they offer a shared temporal language (of the interstice, of the interval) which conjoin drawing and film as expanded and transformed modes, always pushing, always testing the edges, insisting upon an irregular pulse that animates both the drawn line and the filmic still.

Many aspects of Ogunji's work are informed by her impressions of living and working in Lagos, Nigeria. The artist is continually drawn to what the Nigerian megacity offers her practice. As a city it has a combination of unlimited access to everything and many people striving for basic, elemental survival. This tension produces moments of intense beauty and humanity, in Ogunji's view, as well as operating as a leveller of experience. Even very wealthy people sometimes have to think about basic survival (for example during losses of power or water scarcity). There is a sensation of collective humanity there, which she sees as distinct to her experience of growing up in the United States. Ogunji's work is occupied with notions of a shared humanity, but also with the prospect of a super-humanity, beyond reality. This interest links her practice to the work of Nidhal Chamekh and David Musgrave, and their varying approaches to drawing as a technology able to manifest something beyond the human, its gestures and pulse points. Ogunji has observed that her drawings are trying to articulate something for which the language doesn't yet exist; a formulation that reiterates this reach beyond the prosaic limits of the human body and its capacity for language.

In the tautness of her drawings, space is always layered, even when it is seemingly empty in its expansiveness. There is a correlation here to other exhibiting artists who leave large expanses of blank paper in their drawings, including ruby onyinyechi amanze, Massinissa Selmani and Barbara Walker. In Ogunji's work, there is often a relationship to the sea, the Atlantic Ocean in particular representing an interstitial space between the African and American continents. It is visualised on a poetic and metaphoric level: the sense of an almost unimaginable vastness, in which the paper becomes like the sea – a wide, open expanse that can change at any moment. The paper/ink material variance between land and sea witnessed in Prendergast's *Atlas* enables a similar operation of abstraction, in its commitment to openness, movement, and circulatory systems. In considering drawing's nomadic presence and present, cartography becomes a necessary condition for the body's itinerant fields of occupation.

As feminist philosopher Rosi Braidotti has proposed, 'nomadic thought amounts to a politically invested cartography of the present condition of mobility in a globalized world.'[15] Braidotti's important theoretical framework of 'nomadic thought,' which I wish to transfer to the material realm of 'nomadic drawing,' is centred on finding new ways of articulating our complex and contradictory identities as global citizens, post-globalisation. It attempts to find various means of expressing such mobile feminist subjectivities, eschewing fixed perspectives in favour of intersecting social and political positions. Braidotti argues that: 'A cartography is a theoretically based and politically informed reading of the present. A cartographic approach fulfils the function of providing both analytic and exegetical

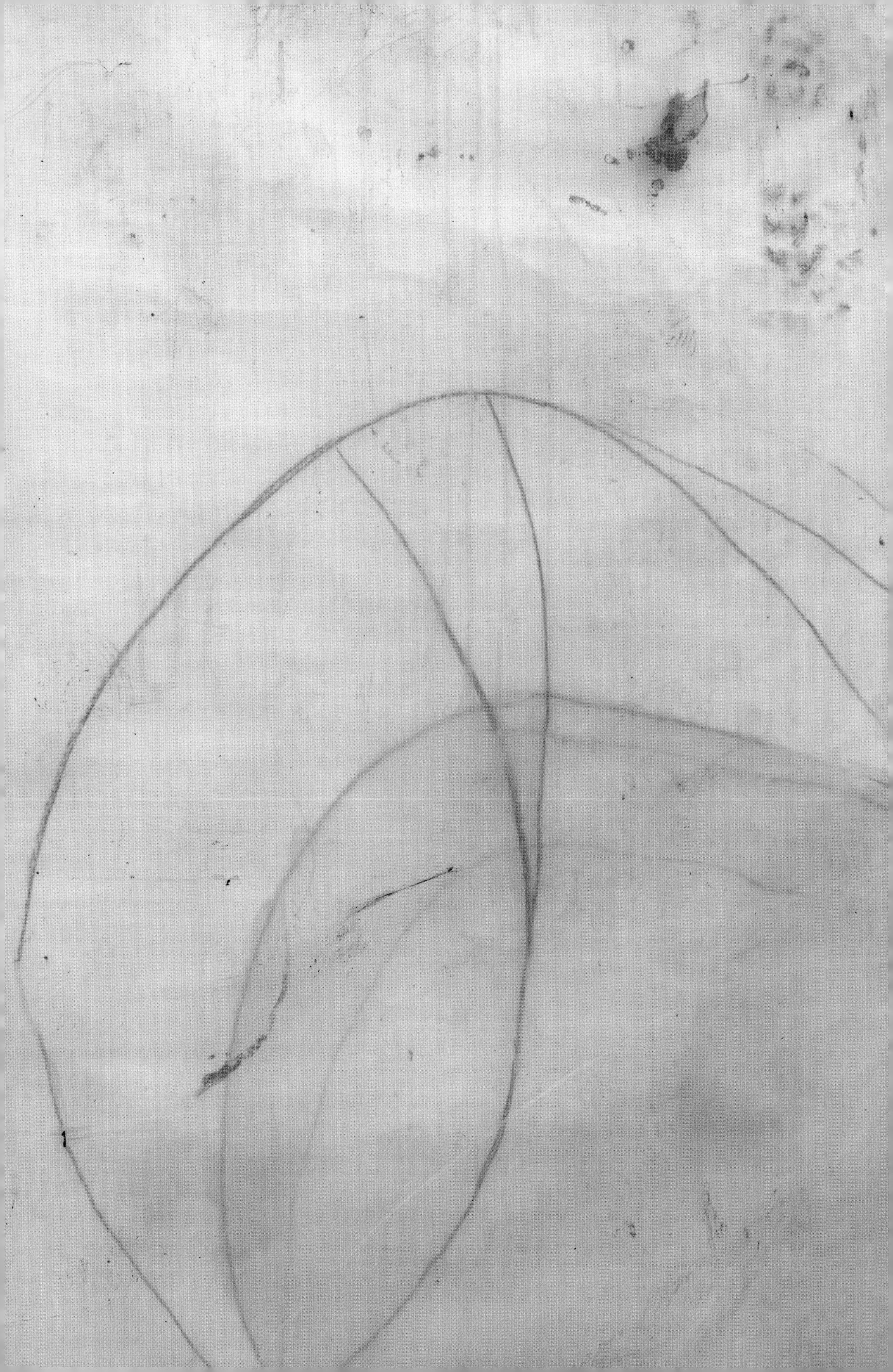

tools for critical thought and also creative theoretical alternatives.'[16] Considering a cartographic approach to nomadic drawing, as already witnessed in Prendergast's and Ogunji's practices, offers a rethinking of the boundaries of contemporary drawing, without losing sight of its embrace of material specificity.

As model; as fragment

As previously suggested, the 'specifics' of drawing (in both a material and theoretical sense) are strengthened, rather than diluted, by its contemporary intermedial alignment. A very different spatial exploration of nomadic drawing grounded by intermediality can be seen in the work of Ian Kiaer, whose long-term installation-based projects respond to the fragmented narratives of utopian modernist thinkers and architects, like Bruno Taut and Frederick Kiesler. The common thread that connects Kiaer's historical subjects is their resistance to the dominant ideologies of their time, in favour of radical – and even impossible – methods of relating to the world. Kiaer's interest in retrieving various manifestations of utopian thinking and research echoes the potential of drawing to operate as a way of seeing and indeed *re-seeing* the world. In Kiaer's architectural/archival splices, the body's (and the subject's) relationship to their environment is explored through the politics of the fragment and the view (be that aerial or close-up). His work is particularly concerned with how the

model (or diagram, or fragment) intersects with the haptic traces of human interaction provoked by physical surroundings (such as the boredom triggered by waiting at a bus stop, manifested through the scoring or writing accumulated on the Plexiglas sheets of the shelter's advertising hoardings). Drawing is visible, not as an image per se, but rather as a faint intervention on an already made, painted or found surface: it might articulate a plan, a model, a doodle or scribble. In each case, it is fragmentary and uncertain. Reflecting on how the idea of the model operates in his practice, Kiaer has said:

> There was an energy in the amount of ideas that could be contained in such an abbreviated form, and although quite makeshift, there was also a delicacy and an attention to the tone of each proposition. [...] there was something distinctive about the unease that these models could achieve while still remaining informal.[17]

While not wishing to invoke designations of the provisional or preliminary in relation to drawing, there is something revealed here about drawing's relationship to abbreviation, informality and intimacy (notions all interrogated and reworked by Kiaer). This underscores the cartographic as a methodology of bodily irruption, confronting our understanding of the world via both 'analytical and exegetical tools,' as Braidotti phrases it; the very function of an endnote, as most of Kiaer's works are titled.

Ian Kiaer
Endnote, tooth, 2017 (detail)
Plexiglas, charcoal, pencil and varnish on paper, plastic, fan,
dimensions variable

following spread
Ian Kiaer
Endnote, tooth (panoramico, canopy), 2017
Plexiglas, acrylic, varnish and pencil on paper

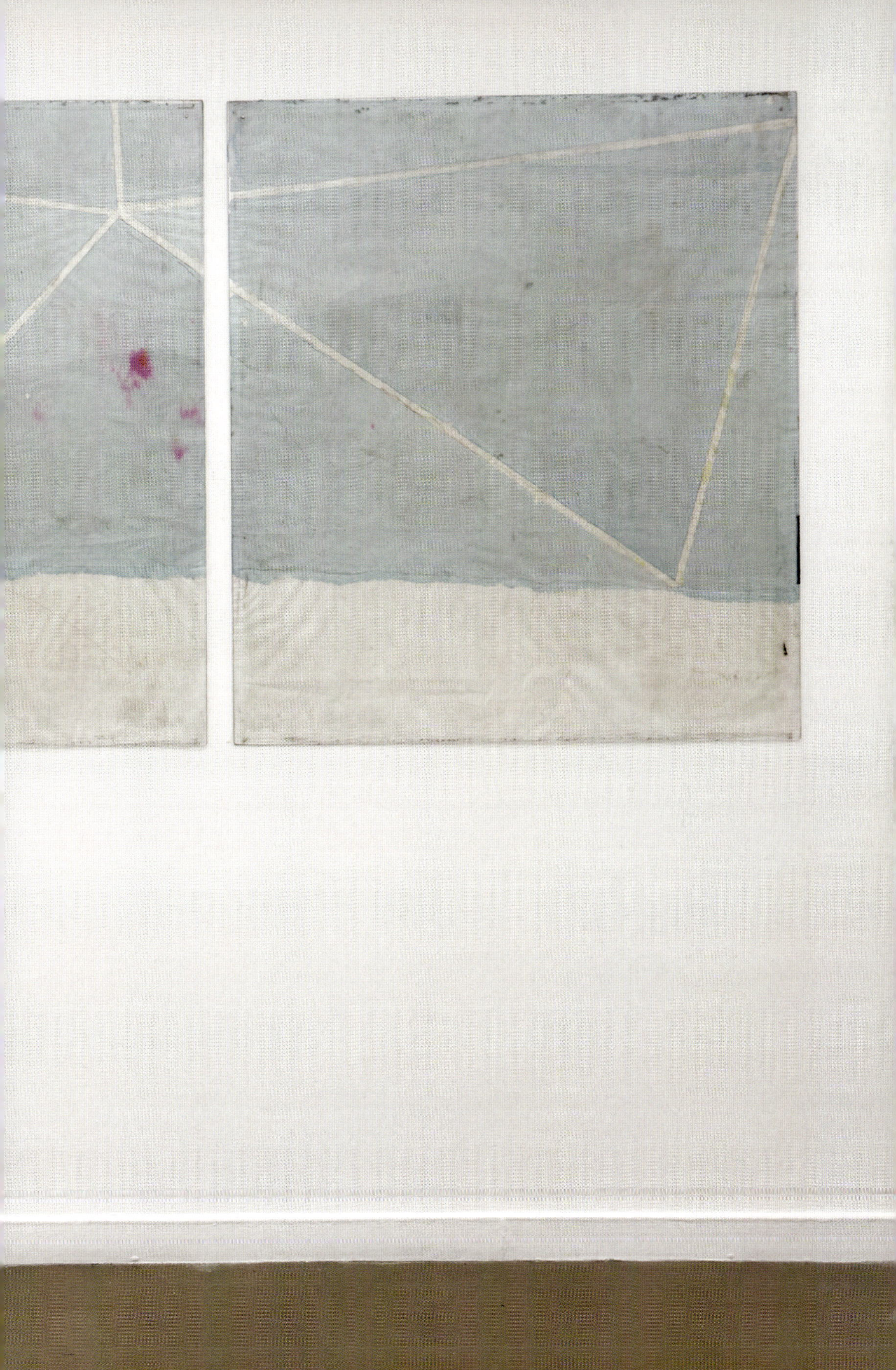

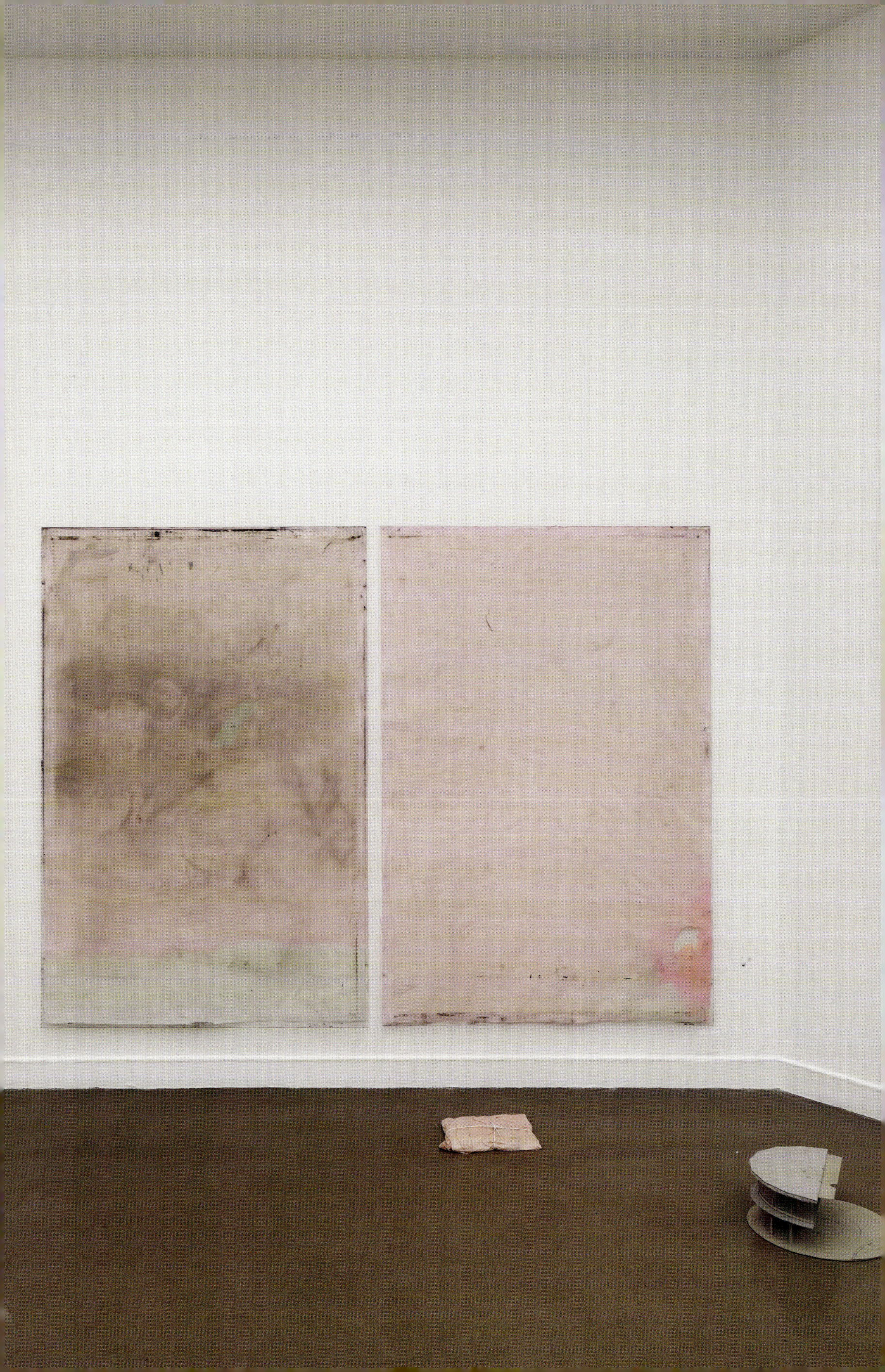

For Kiaer's three-part paper and Plexiglas sheet work *Endnote, tooth (panoramico, canopy)* (pp.30–31), a related installation's accompanying architectural model (p.32), and the video *Endnote, tooth* (all 2017), the subject is in each case a panoramic building overlooking Lisbon: the Monsanto restaurant designed by Chaves da Costa in 1968 (located next to a military barracks, and somewhat associated with the Portuguese 'New State' dictatorship of 1933–74). This deeply politicised building offers the panoramic view as a manifestation of power. Abandoned since 2002, and now operating as an anti-authoritarian site of drug dealing and taking, the restaurant is, in Kiaer's words, an artificial monument to the past, operating and existing in multiple tenses (past, present and future). The building exists now as a shell of the viewing platform, no longer fully itself, not yet fully a ruin. It is, the artist suggests, like a working model.

In *Endnote, tooth* (detail, p.28), three large sheets of paper are separated from the viewer by bus stop advertising panels. Incredibly stained, marked and discoloured, they completely alter our perception of the white paper underneath. The panels contain different registers of mark making, the artist's marks and others, the temporality of dirt and the passage of time. The interventions by waiting bus passengers act as readymade graphic incisions that are almost unintentional; tedium-induced scrawls rather than purposeful graffiti. The two layers of information, paper and Plexiglas, offer us

diverging, fragmentary glimpses into a moment that is suspended between the artist's studio and the street. Like many operations within drawing, Kiaer explains that: 'The way a fragment works is to draw attention to what isn't there whilst remaining very specific in itself. In that way, a work can be kept open and asks an investment of imagination from the viewer that they may not want to give.'[18] This experimental openness – emerging from the dialogue between artist and viewer – is vital to nomadic drawing practices. Nomadism accepts its relationship to not knowing; to the inchoate image that emerges from the self-reflexive slowness of drawing.

Kiaer's practice encourages a creative conflict between knowledge that is derived from measurement (such as an architectural plan of a building) and knowledge that is derived from the environment (the spatial experience of said building in its locale). The model enables the coexistence of both forms: as a not-quite concrete proposition, its perspective is adaptable. The architectural historian Beatriz Colomina has argued that: 'To think about modern architecture must be to pass back and forth between the question of space and the question of representation.'[19] This is the passageway between environment and measurement that Kiaer's practice traverses, and in its subject/object dialectic, this formulation has an equal bearing on the work of another artist in the exhibition, Milano Chow.

If the 'house is a frame for a view,' as Colomina also proposes in *Privacy and Publicity: Modern Architecture as Mass Media*, then what Chow's precise graphite and photo-transfer drawings offer is a tension-filled yet elegant stand off between architecture-as-frame and the body-as-framed. We are the viewing subjects, turned back against architecture's outwards view, in favour of the house-as-object.

As transfer

There are two categories of photography in this exhibition: the first in which the photographic image is directly transferred (using solvents) to the paper's surface, and the second in which the image is re-drawn by hand, from photographic source to graphite rendering. Milano Chow, ruby onyinyechi amanze and Nidhal Chamekh's *Le Battement des Ailes* series all explore fragmentary uses of the photo transfer process; whereas artists Kate Davis, Karl Haendel, David Haines, Massinissa Selmani and Barbara Walker copy historical, archival or digitally-sourced photographs to produce their highly-skilled graphite drawings (explored in Kate Macfarlane's essay, 'Drawing as Thinking through Material Encounter').

Three works by Chow (all 2017, pp.35–37) contain multiple frames, borders and objects: a *mise-en-abyme* of architectural, interior design and fashion detailing. Doorways, ornate cornices, windows, columns, mirrors – even plug sockets – all confuse our sense of what is interior or exterior space. Scale oscillates, too: what looks like detailed plaster work around the drawings' perimeters offer close-up pattern work in contrast to the larger scale of the objects they frame. This intentional play with pastiche and ironic distance in Chow's drawing practice invites a celebration of artificiality. This stance underscores the relationship to Los Angeles (where she lives and works) visible in her drawings: like artist Ed Ruscha, whose works first emerged on the LA art scene of the early 1960s, the viewer does not see any evidence of the artist's hand or visible drawing gestures. The surface sheen of LA, and its relationship to the artificiality of filmmaking, is palpable in Chow's world. In Ruscha's case, the space of drawing becomes a stage set, or a well-lit photography studio, twisting traditional medium and genre categories to produce uncertain and unreal effects.[20] Similarly, Chow's intermedial sensibility is underpinned by the artifice of her chosen spaces, which, akin to film sets or department store window displays, are really shallow slivers or *slices* of space; membranes between outside and inside, like doors and windows. As she notes: 'It's not important for me to specify the exact visual or historical references in each work – they're more about using the language of architecture, diagrams, picturemaking, etc…'[21] This use of multiple visual languages, together finding an unsettling yet picture-perfect home within the intermedial medium of drawing, is predicated

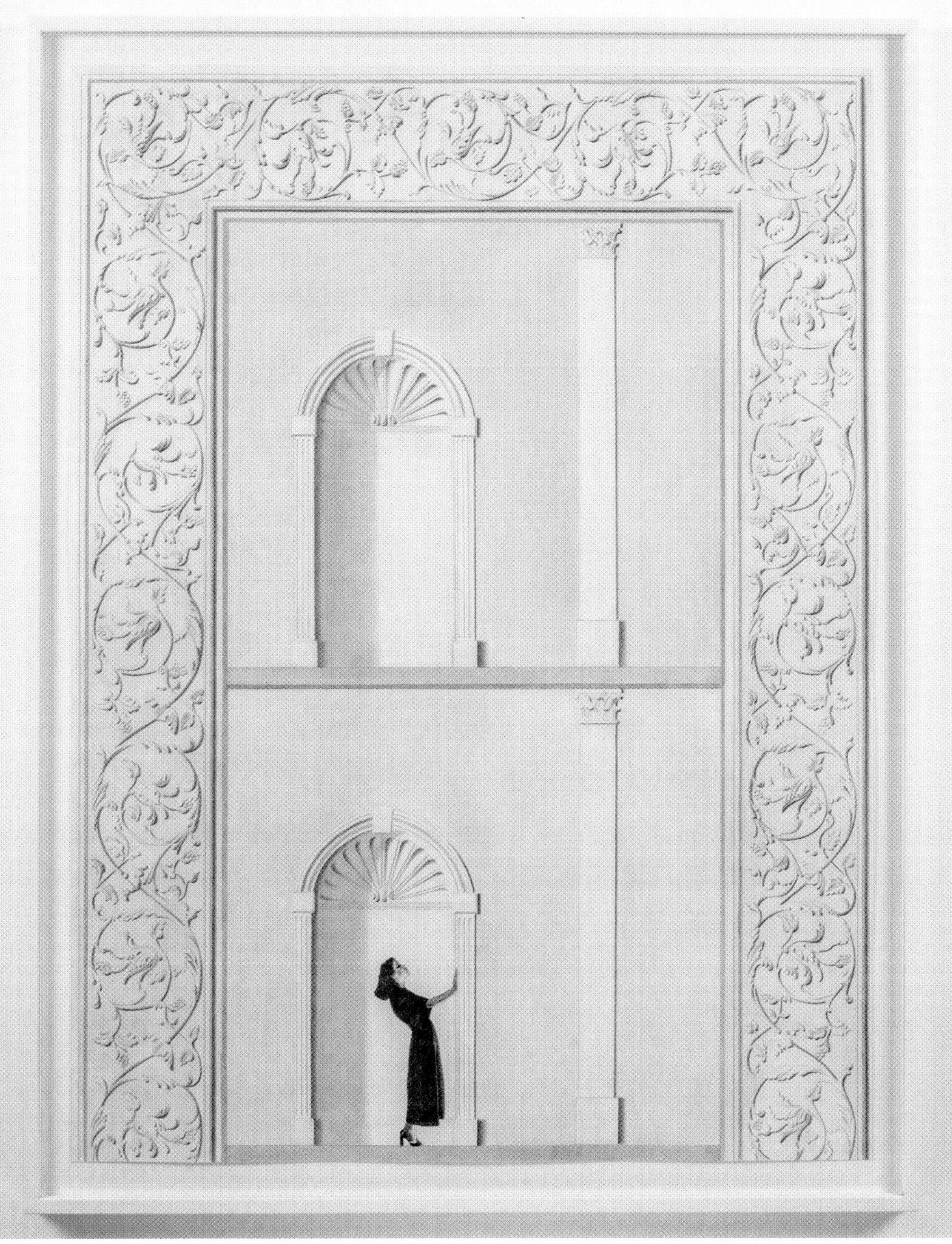

Milano Chow
Entryway (Niches), 2017
Graphite, ink, Flashe and photo transfer on paper, 81.3 × 61 cm

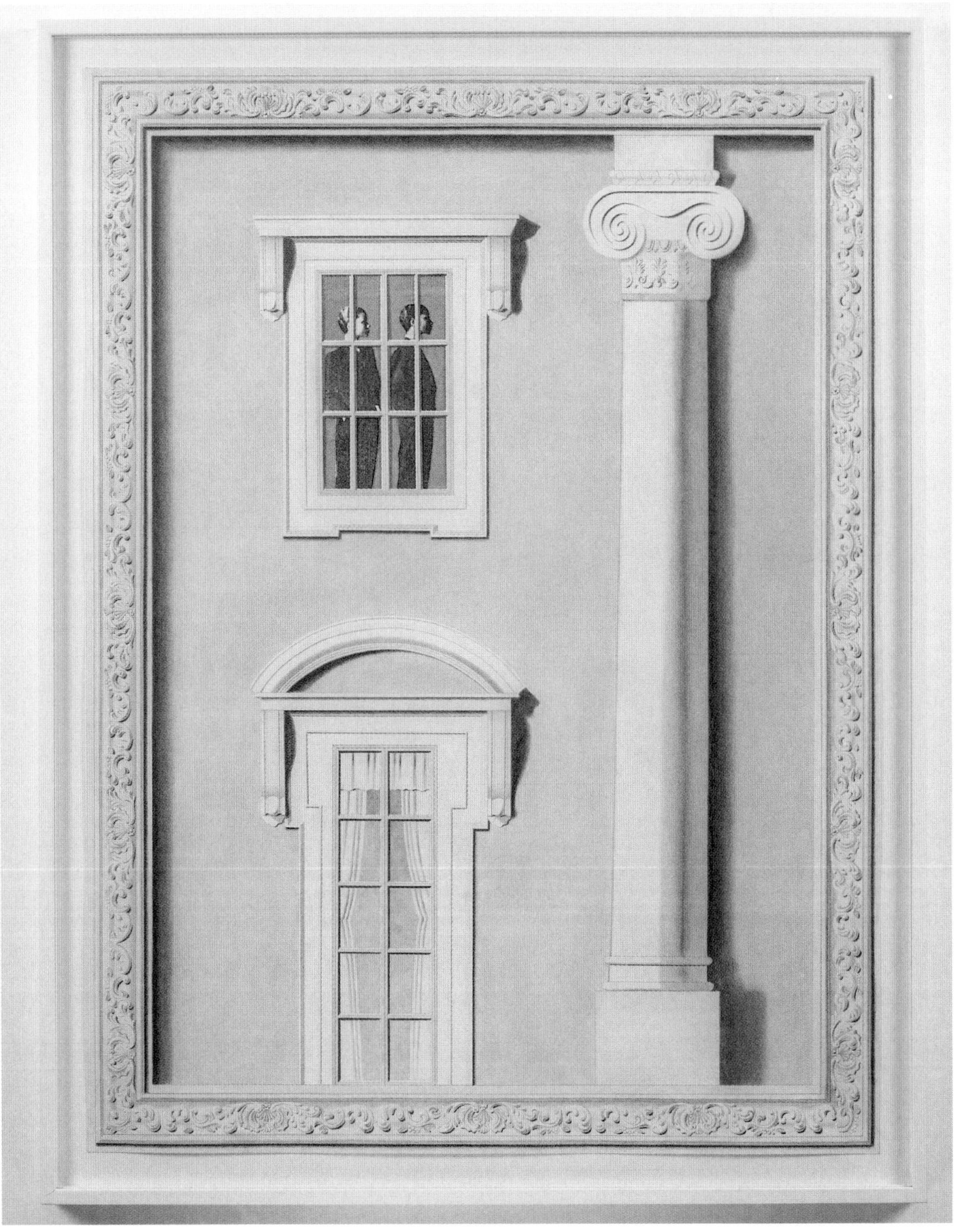

Milano Chow
Frame/Exterior 1, 2017
Graphite, ink, Flashe and photo transfer on paper, 81.3 × 61 cm

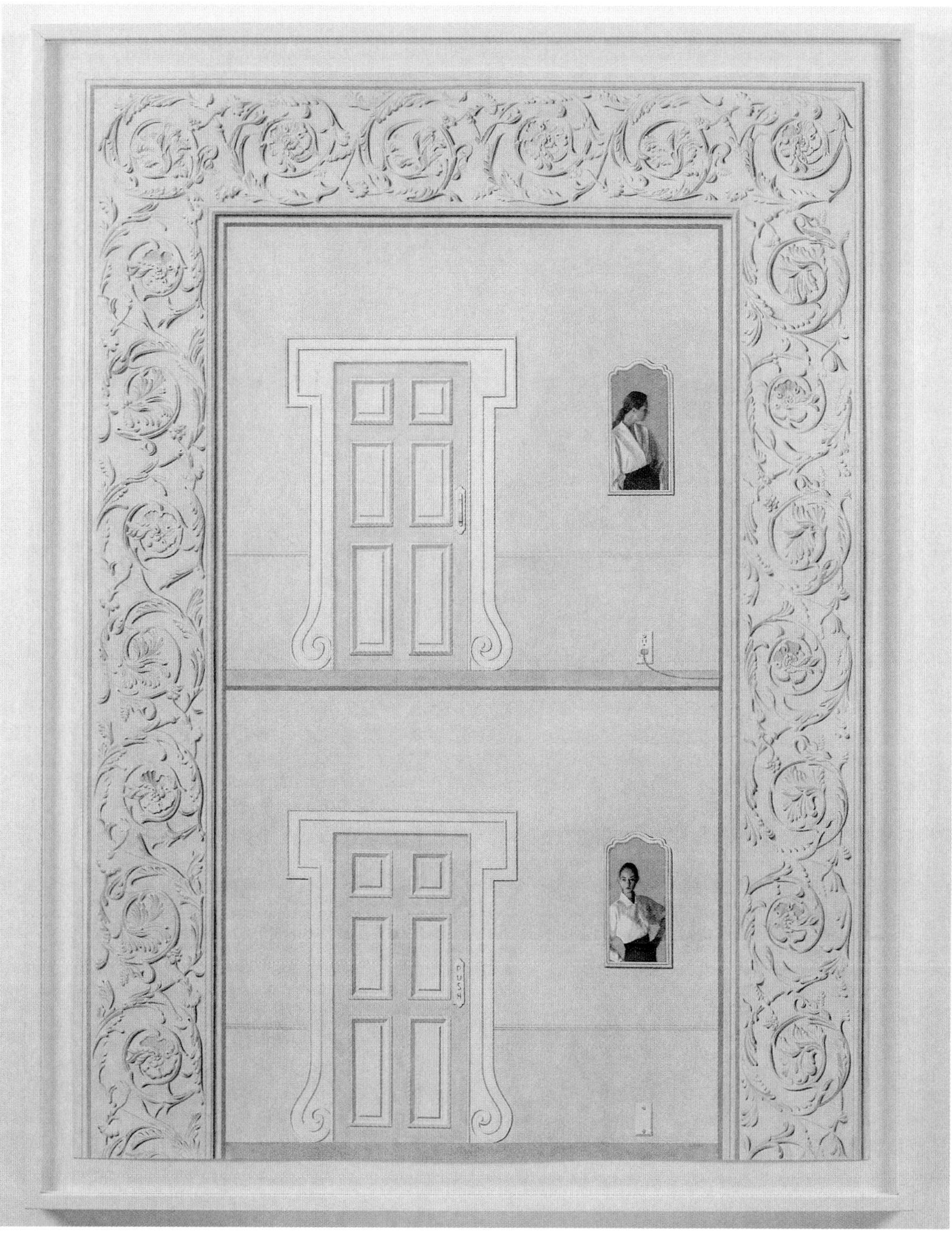

Milano Chow
Entryway (Push/Pull Doors), 2017
Graphite, ink, Flashe and photo transfer on paper, 81.3 × 61 cm

on a continuously smooth and seamless movement. This movement maps the nomadic mobility of Chow's references and figurations.

The people that appear within these frames studiously avoid looking at us, their viewers. With their gazes carefully averted, they maintain the elegant yet stiff poses of models, producing sharp clothing lines and silhouettes, presenting themselves as products to be consumed. This question of the gaze is not solely an embodied one, in the context of architectural space. Returning to Colomina, we find that: 'The picture window works in two ways: it turns the outside world into an image to be consumed by those inside the house, but it also displays the image of the interior to the outside world.'[22] This voracious, bilateral consumption of images could apply to the wider field of contemporary drawing, too.

The people in Chow's work are its *undrawn* element: they are conjured from photo-transferred images sourced in fashion magazines or advertisements; their precise origins wilfully uncertain. In Chow's practice, which she describes as 'figures in imagined architecture,' her drawing works to contain, isolate and make strange these photo-transferred figures.[23] Chow, together with amanze and Chamekh, deploy the photo transfer as a contagion within their drawing practices. It operates as a foreign body whose presence actually strengthens the vitality of its host.

As art historian Ed Krčma writes of Robert Rauschenberg's transfer drawings, *Thirty-Four Illustrations for Dante's Inferno* (1958–60): 'the transfer method represents a withering of drawing's chief competencies: its assimilation and translation of perceptual and imaginative experience into graphic form; its practised and dexterous handling of instruments; and the cultivation of its fluid responsiveness to the shifts in bodily and psychological intensity.'[24] What we have in this series, Krčma demonstrates, is Rauschenberg 'reconfiguring drawing as a technological hybrid,' rather than as a medium defined (and delimited) by its specificity and recurring pedagogical frameworks.[25]

With these three artists' contemporary use of the photo transfer, we may perceive a further evolution of this notion of drawing as 'technological hybrid,' an evolution that Krčma tracks with reference to the 'hybrid forms of drawing' that have emerged since the late 1980s and early 1990s: 'Such practices have engaged drawing's technological condition while insisting upon both the critical value and enabling resistances of its material conditions.'[26] This dialectic of the technological and material conditions of drawing is what ruby onyinyechi amanze synthesises in her large-scale series 'aliens, hybrids and ghosts' (2013–ongoing).

As amanze's artist statement explains: 'In a non-linear and open narrative, [these] drawings explore space as a malleable construct, the freedom to play as an act of revolution,

ruby onyinyechi amanze
astroturf rooftop picnics (Lagos), ghana must go (bags) somewhere, anywhere – overweight luggage unpacked at airport counters, isn't a chandelier like a plant? a delicate semblance of permanence. neon hearts. we all have them, 2015 (detail)
Photo transfers, collage, ink, metallic pigment, graphite and coloured pencil on paper, 182.9 × 303.5 cm

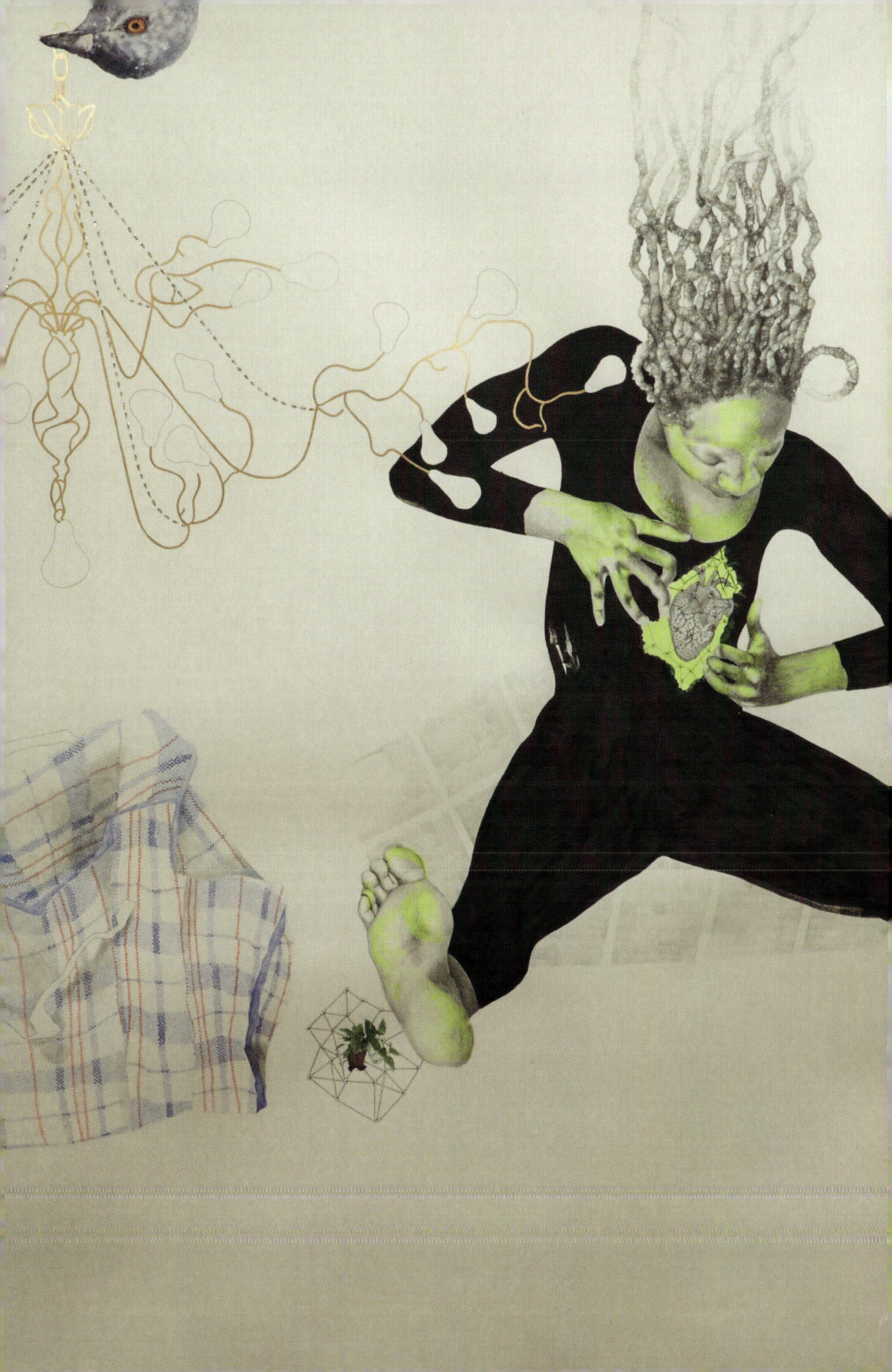

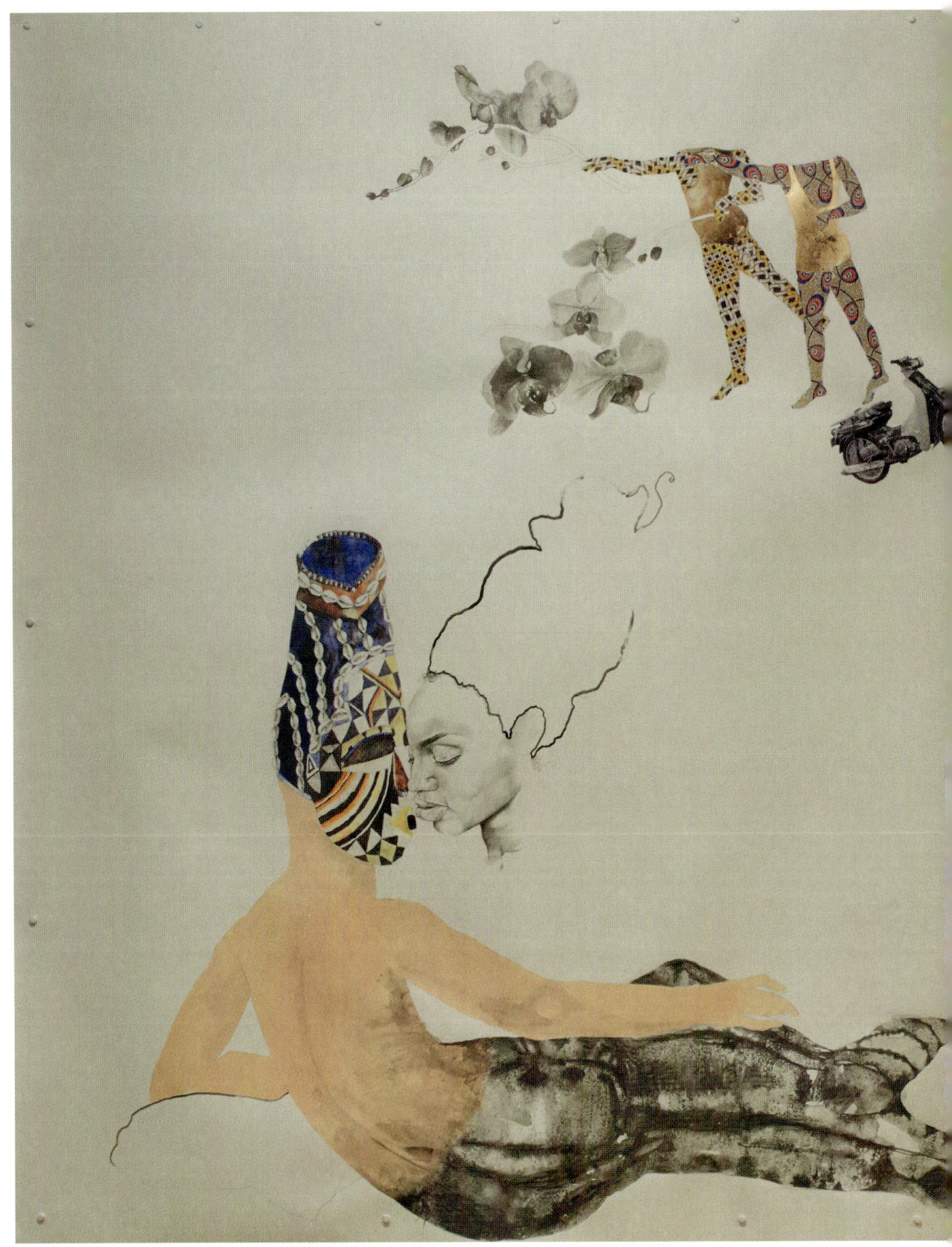

ruby onyinyechi amanze

that low hanging kind of sun, the one that lingers two feet above your head,
(never dying) house plants in exchange for your freedom… orchids in exchange
for your love, who are you kissing, when you kiss a mask?, 2015
Photo transfers, collage, ink, metallic pigment, graphite and coloured
pencil on paper, 182.9 × 301.6 cm

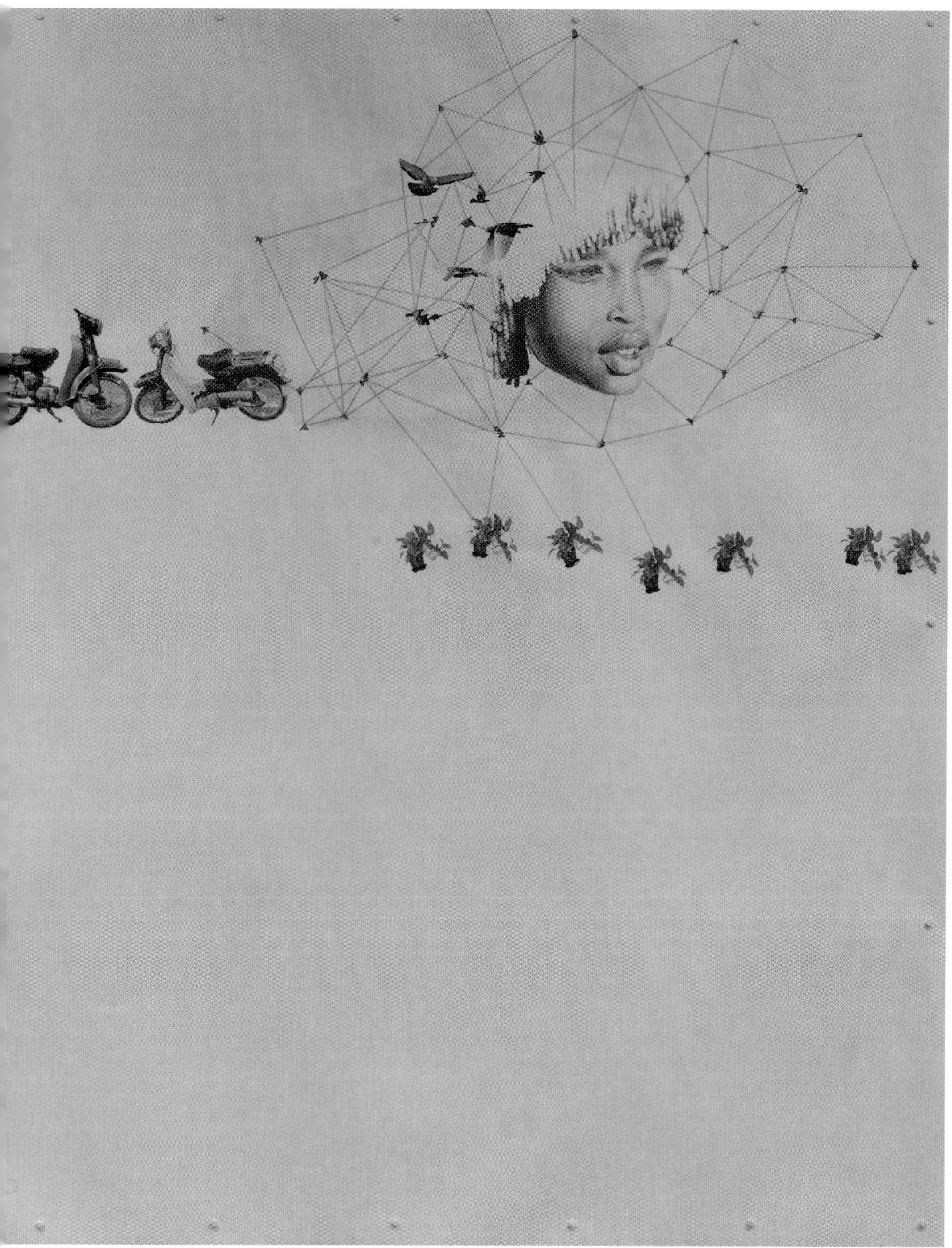

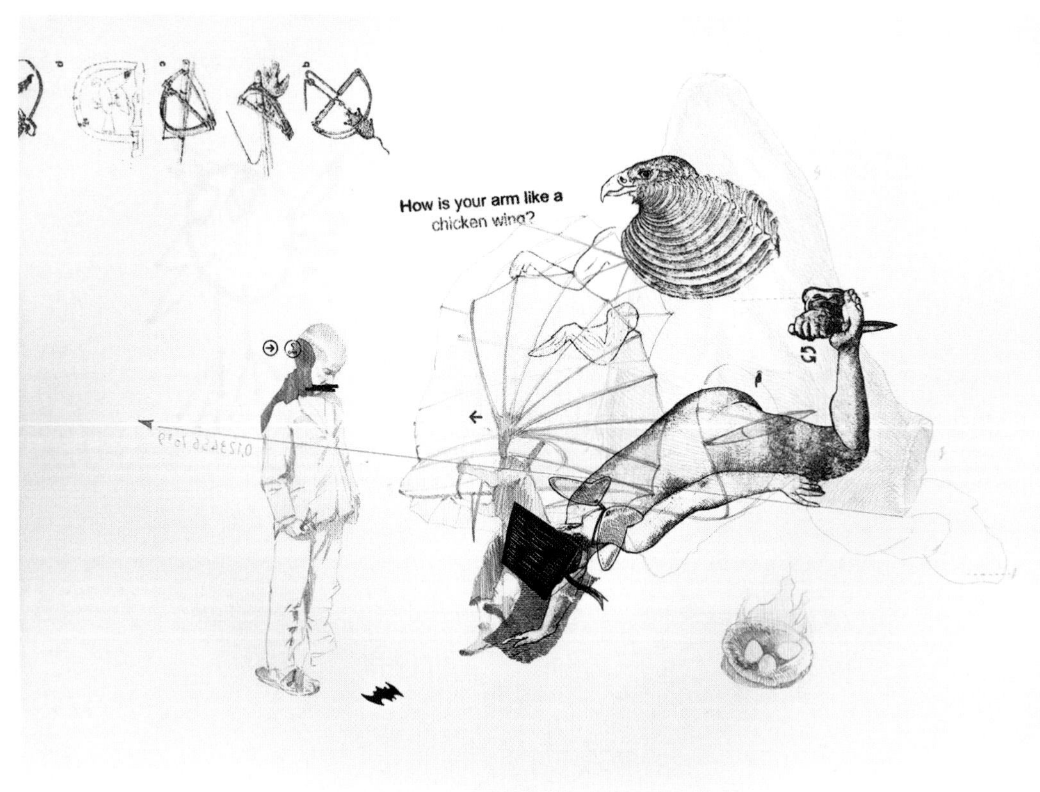

Nidhal Chamekh
Le Battement des Ailes No.XVI, 2017
Graphite, ink, transfer on cotton paper, 23 × 32.5 cm

and cultural hybridity or "post-colonial non-nationalism" as a mundane norm.'[27] *that low hanging kind of sun, the one that lingers two feet above your head, (never dying) house plants in exchange for your freedom… orchids in exchange for your love, who are you kissing, when you kiss a mask?* (2015, pp. 39–41) belongs to this series. Its vast expanse of paper surface includes collaged and photo-transferred elements, as well as drawing in graphite, ink, coloured pencils and metallic pigments. On her use of photo transfer, amanze comments: 'Unlike with collage where the image sits on top of the page, photo transfer become part of the paper. It's the thinnest application of ink on the surface. There are some things I chose to transfer instead of draw. I don't think drawing should pretend to be photography. If I need a photographic image, I'll just use one.'[28]

The global, postcolonial and culturally hybrid existence that amanze expresses with a desire to be considered as merely a 'mundane norm' is reflected in her materially hybrid strategy for drawing. The genesis of the 'aliens, hybrids and ghosts' series can be traced to her time in Nigeria in 2012, when she undertook a Fulbright Scholarship to Nsukka: 'It's inspired by my own story of being a nomad and having multiple homes, and not ever fitting neatly into a box of where I'm from or how I identify […] It's celebrating that middle space, considering it be an authentic space as opposed to one of dislocation.'[29] By overlaying multiple geographically and temporally distinct zones within this 'middle' space of her works on paper, amanze's nomadic drawing pivots around the authenticity – and inherent freedoms – of such a fragmented and contradictory utopia.

Nidhal Chamekh's series *Le Battement des Ailes* assembles complex superimposed layers of graphic signs and symbols, both iconic and indexical, utilising photo transfer, ink and graphite against empty white space. All of the visual components in this series are sourced from archives. There is a focus on structural and anatomical comparisons between human and animal bodies, and a further link suggested between the state of humanity (on both an ethical and epistemological level) and the state of our planet. Ultimately, the wider universe is put into play, leading to suggestive notions of alien/human hybridity and the transformative potential of the alien (in all the many and varied interpretations of that term), as also seen in amanze's drawings.[30] In *Les Battement des Ailes D* (2017, pp.44–45), the two detailed images of a man's head, seen face on and in profile, are sourced from photographs taken by Dutch scientists who came to 'study' the populations of North Africa, with the attendant colonial implications of observation, control and the animal-like treatment of their human subjects such historic research studies imply.

Le Battement des Ailes translates as 'beating of the wings.' In Chamekh's view, the phrase also refers to the struggle of birds trying to escape, to find flight when their wings are bound, and

following spread
Nidhal Chamekh
Le Battement des Ailes D, 2017
Inks, graphite and transfer on cotton paper, 100 × 140 cm

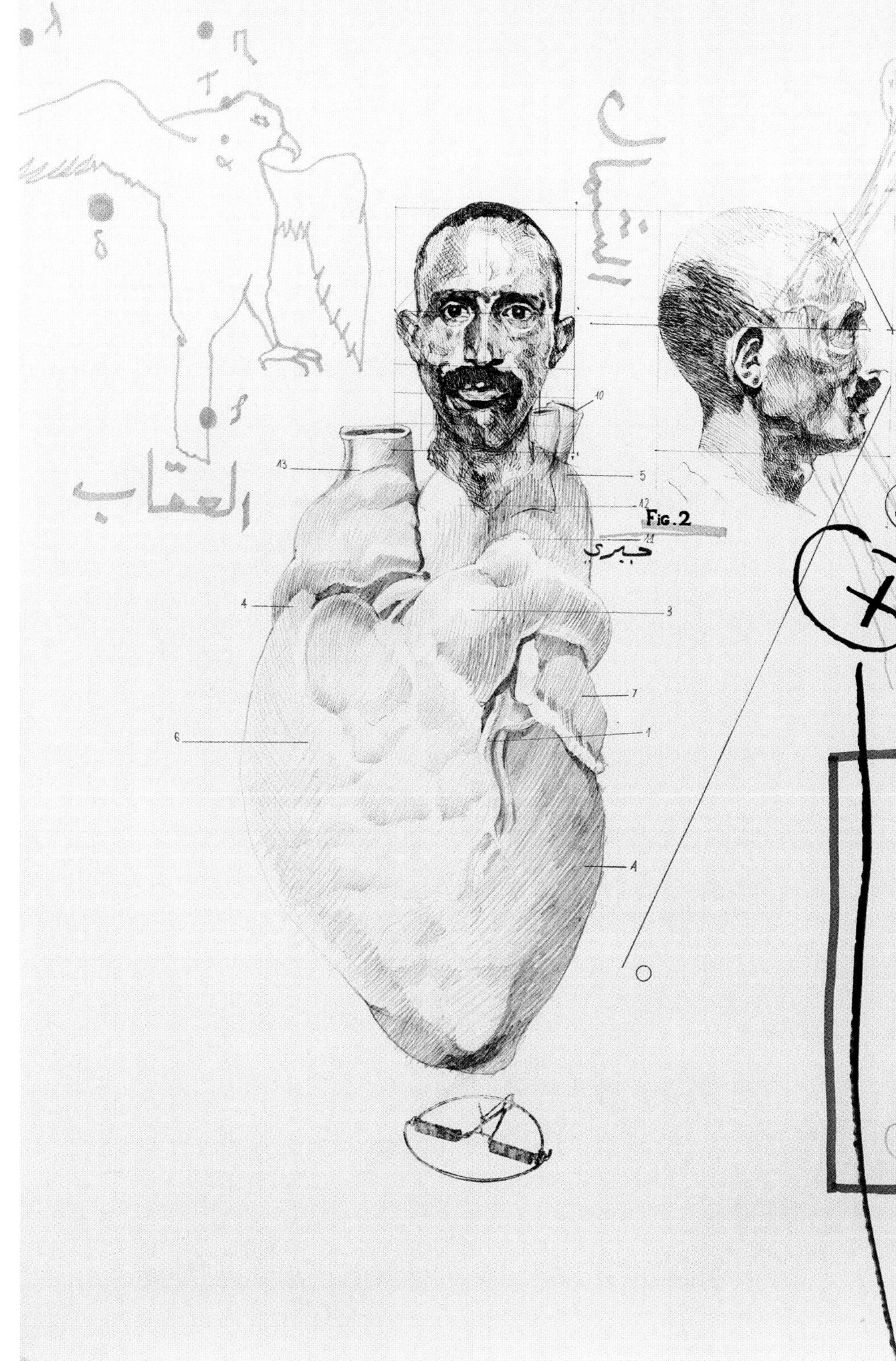

العقاب
النسر
حبيبي
Fig.2
A
B
C
O
13
10
5
12
11
3
4
6
7
1
A

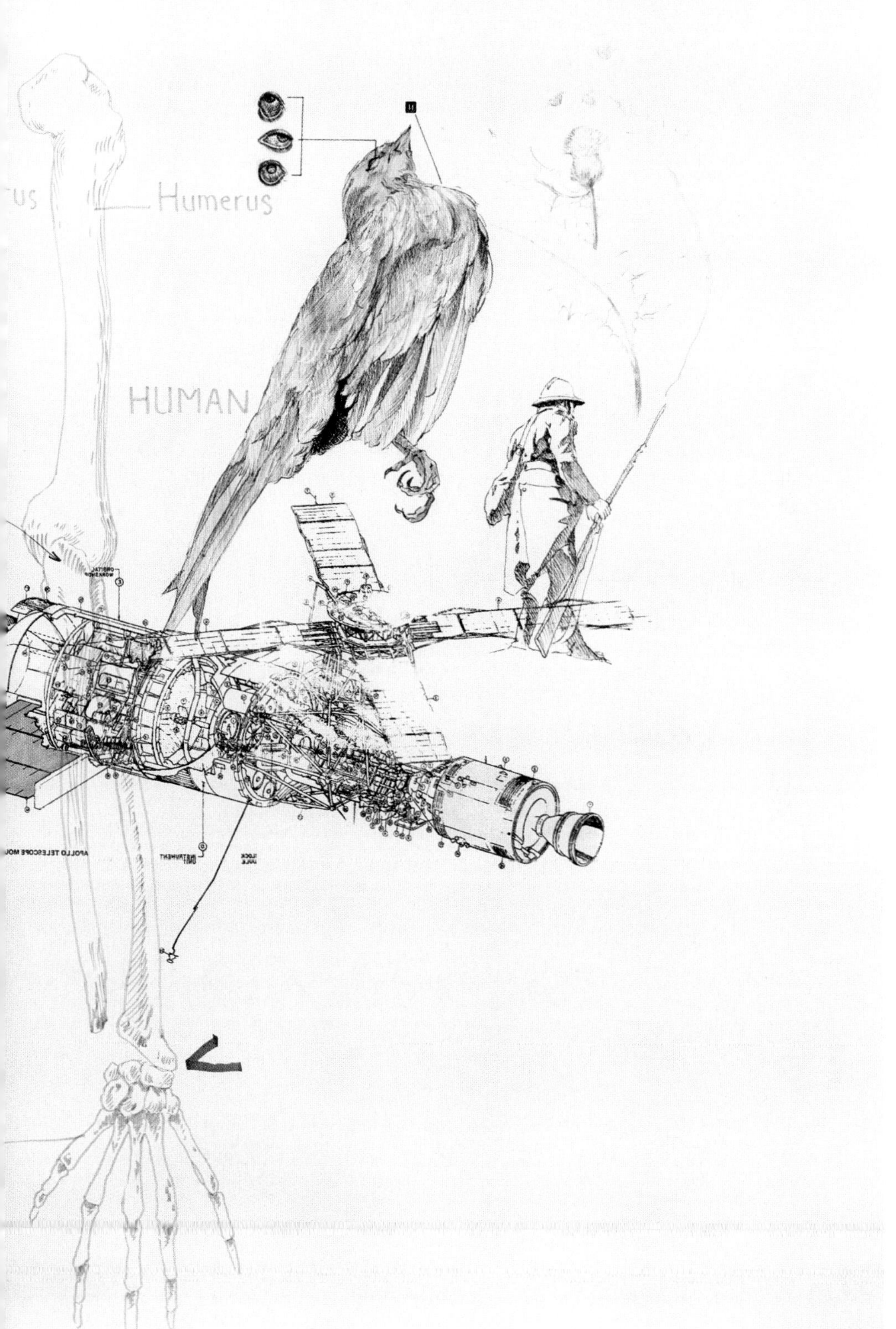

Humerus
HUMAN

to humans in a position of struggle – both physical and political. There is a freedom that Chamekh locates in the work's multiple references, which offer new perspectives on reality, often approached from an imaginary or fantastical viewpoint. The drawing creates an imaginary and imaginative space from the juxtaposition of incredibly different source materials, which cannot logically be connected. The series is characterised by this dramatic mise-en-scène: a montage of historical images, notations, diagrams and inventions. We lost something with modernity's rationality, the artist implies with this series. The relentless focus on evidentiary fact lost sight of the potential for other associative links to be found within a nomadic, temporal space of ambiguity and transformation. We are never able to truly understand the present without the past: Chamekh insists on this; as we must all do.

These artists who continue to reimagine the boundaries and borders of contemporary drawing remain invested in its material specificity. This duality of an enduring yet nomadic image of drawing is produced from our collective (and often contentious) mobility in a globalised world. Cartographic methods provide us with the tools to navigate drawing's nomadic time and space, while implicating the body in cartography's processes of registration and figuration. This essay has charted various articulations of impossible spaces, which bring together inherently contradictory ideas, subject positions, histories and bodies. Here drawing is dramatised as a space of modelling, of montage and of transfer, reliant on fragmented narratives and the staging of 'otherness' and displacement. These artists' use of multiple visual languages within drawing only strengthens this nomadic energy. In arguing that the simple act of drawing with pencil on paper should be understood as a technology, what we come to realise is that today's mediated, de-centred and interactive image technologies have given new agency to this solitary material pursuit, to drawing's past and present.

Stephanie Straine

1   The exhibition dates at the Museum of Modern Art Oxford for *[Drawing]* were 18 November – 23 December 1972, later extended to 7 January 1973.

2   Andrew Hutton, 'Avant-Garde Survey', in *Oxford Mail*, 20 December 1972.

3   Acknowledgements, *[Drawing]* exhibition catalogue, the Museum of Modern Art Oxford, 1972, unpaginated. Modern Art Oxford archive.

4   What came to be labelled as conceptual art was never really about 'disappearance,' least of all the disappearance of the object. However, the still persistent notion of the 'dematerial' began with Lucy Lippard and John Chandler's article 'The dematerialisation of art,' *Art International* (12:2) in February 1968, pp.31–36, and was later expanded into Lippard's illustrated bibliography of conceptual art, *Six Years: The Dematerialization of the Art Object from 1966 to 1972*, London and New York, 1973. Regarding dematerialisation, more recently many art historians have attempted to disrupt the misleading hegemony of this term. For an excellent reappraisal see the book review by Anna Dezeuze, 'Dealing with Dematerialization,' in *Art History*, Vol. 32, No. 2 (2009), pp.399–404.

5   *[Drawing]* private view invitation, Modern Art Oxford archive, *[Drawing]* folder, 1972 box.

6   Lucy Steeds, 'Exhibitions [of Drawings] in Britain, 1964–80,' in *Towards Visibility: Exhibiting Contemporary Drawing 1964–80*, Paris, 2015, p.56.

7   Sections of this essay are adapted from my unpublished PhD thesis, *The Ground of Drawing: Graphic Operations in the 1960s and 1970s*, University College London, 2013.

8   The term 'drawing in the expanded field' was proposed by Anna Lovatt and Ed Krčma with reference to Rosalind Krauss's 'Sculpture in the Expanded Field,' in *October*, Vol. 8 (Spring 1979), pp.30–44. Lovatt and Krčma, 'Drawing in the Expanded Field' conference session, Association of Art Historians Conference 2009, Manchester Metropolitan University. For an exploration of this expanded or 'extended' field of drawing, see Catherine de Zegher, 'A Century under the Sign of Line: Drawing and its Extension (1910 –2010),' in *On Line: Drawing through the Twentieth Century*, eds. Cornelia Butler and Catherine de Zegher (exh. cat., The Museum of Modern Art), New York, 2010.

9   Lars Ellström, ed., *Media Borders, Multimodality and Intermediality*, Basingstoke and New York, 2010, p.4.

10 Tania Kovats, *Drawing Water*, The Fruitmarket Gallery, Edinburgh, 2014, p.11.

11 Wura-Natasha Ogunji: 'More recently I have become interested in the drawing as an object. One thing I have always loved about this trace paper is that it moves. You can see it especially in the larger work. The flow of air in a gallery moves them. It's a slow, measured kind of movement, like breathing.'
ruby onyinyechi amanze: 'Given your dual practices of drawing and performance, "paper as body" seems like a lovely way of bridging the two.'
ruby onyinyechi amanze and Wura-Natasha Ogunji, 'Paper as Body: A Conversation,' January 2016, https://theoffingmag.com/enumerate/paper-as-body/

12 Author's notes from studio visit with Kathy Prendergast, 18 January 2018, London.

13 Ogunji observes that her threads are never made into a fabric, so the work is not equivalent to the process of making a textile that has a singular woven surface and structure. In her practice, the threads remain unwoven, unbound, and unstable. She is not comfortable with the equation between sewing, embroidery, and women's work. In Nigeria, it is the men who do the embroidery. It is a very simplistic reduction to equate textiles (or even the suggestion of them) with the feminine. Notes adapted from the author's conversation with Wura-Natasha Ogunji, 13 January 2018, Berlin.

14 Notes adapted from the author's conversation with Wura-Natasha Ogunji, 13 January 2018, Berlin.

15 Rosi Braidotti, *Nomadic Subjects: Embodiment and Sexual Difference in Contemporary Feminist Theory*, New York, second edition, 2011, p.4.

16 Ibid., p.4.

17 Ian Kiaer, 'Interview with Ian Kiaer and Caoimhín Mac Giolla Léith,' in *Ian Kiaer: Endless House Projects* (exh. cat., The British School at Rome), Rome, 2006, p.19.

18 Ibid., p.21.

19 Beatriz Colomina, *Privacy and Publicity: Modern Architecture as Mass Media*, Cambridge, Mass., and London, 1994, p.13. With thanks to Milano Chow for drawing my attention to this publication.

20 For further analysis of Ed Ruscha's drawing practice and its relationship to Los Angeles, see my forthcoming essay 'Drawing's Finish' in *A Companion to Contemporary Drawing*, eds. Kelly Chorpening and Rebecca Fortnum, Wiley Blackwell, 2018.

21 Milano Chow, email to author, 25 February 2018.

22 Colomina 1994, p.8.

23 Milano Chow, email to author, 25 February 2018.

24 Ed Krčma, *Rauschenberg/Dante: Drawing a Modern Inferno*, New Haven, Conn., and London, 2017, p.133.

25 Ibid., p.139.

26 Ibid., p.137.

27 ruby onyinyechi amanze, artist's website, accessed 12 March 2018: http://rubyamanze.com/story

28 ruby onyinyechi amanze, in Katherine McMahon, 'Habitat: ruby onyinyechi amanze,' *Artnews*, 13 August 2015, accessed 15 February 2018: http://www.artnews.com/2015/08/13/habitat-ruby-onyinyechi-amanze/#jp-carousel-52014

29 ruby onyinyechi amanze, artist's website, accessed 12 March 2018: http://rubyamanze.com/story

30 Key points of reference for Chamekh in this drawing series are Deleuze and Guattari on the becoming-animal (*A Thousand Plateaus: Capitalism and Schizophrenia*, 1980, English trans. 1987), and the Hollywood film *Birdy* starring Nicolas Cage (1984, dir. Alan Parker). There is also an important reference to cultural historian Aby Warburg's unfinished *Mnemosyne Atlas*.

DRAWING AS THINKING THROUGH MATERIAL ENCOUNTER

*…put images into circulation, to convey them,
disguise them, deform them, heat them red hot,
freeze them, multiply them*
Michel Foucault[1]

A Slice through the World charts the radical
shift in the status of traditional drawing
techniques since the early 1970s. Conceptual
propositions conveyed through notational
drawings typified those included in the
1972 exhibition *[Drawing]* at the Museum
of Modern Art Oxford.[2] Representational
drawings employing illusionistic techniques
were absent; the organisers viewed such
practices as anti-intellectual and regressive in
their denial of graphic reality and attention
to craft and labour.[3] Yet on the eve of their
obsolescence, avant-garde artists on America's
west coast, such as Ed Ruscha and Vija
Celmins, were reclaiming such illusionistic
techniques as the perfect means to respond
to contemporary life. When in 1975 Foucault
wrote about his regret at the image's loss in
favour of abstraction, he wanted to 'recover
the games of the past,' to set free the sheer
pleasure of playing with images, 'to put images
into circulation, to convey them, disguise
them, deform them, heat them red hot, freeze
them, multiply them'.[4] And later, in 1986,
Robert Longo, the 'Pictures Generation'[5] artist
who employed drawing in the service of
appropriation, stated:

It is very important to understand that they
[the Conceptualists] ripped apart the idea
of art, they were in many ways descendants
of Duchamp, they asked why do you have
things on white walls, why the art object,
etc. It was strange to be the generation
that came after these people, because they
basically left us pictorially with nothing,
maybe the love of the idea.…What
happened is that drawing and painting, that
sort of thing that seemed outmoded and
dead, came back. It seems really radical to
draw, to paint.[6]

For the artists in *A Slice through the World* it
remains radical to incorporate within their
multi-disciplined practices various drawing
techniques that may, in the early 1970s, have
been considered obsolete. Such methodologies
are employed to ask questions – to address not
only *what* we see, but *how* we see. Moreover,
images are utilised as a means to address
the existential question of what it means to
be human. It is interesting to consider in
what ways drawing, specifically, can produce
effective responses to issues at the core of our
existence. Is drawing, in fact, a super-human
medium, despite its basic means: material
traces of physical contact? Can the intense
labour invested in its production counteract
the dehumanised abstraction of the digital
networks that we are forced to negotiate in
our daily lives? This essay further considers
drawing's innately self-reflexive nature: to
translate imagery into a drawing necessarily
involves abstracting from nature.

In *The Pleasure of Drawing* Jean-Luc Nancy talks about drawing in terms of design (*dessein*) – 'the intention to do something deliberately, by design, on purpose.'[7] Each of the artists discussed in this essay employ drawing to mediate imagery and each utilise a material encounter with drawing to articulate a particular concept, though drawing is readily abandoned if an idea is better expressed in another medium such as print, paint, sculpture, animation or film. Under investigation here are drawing modes that employ varying levels of skill, labour and finish, from hyperrealism in the drawing of David Haines, photorealism as employed by Karl Haendel and in works discussed here rejected by Kate Davis, trompe l'oeil in work by David Musgrave, chiaroscuro and *sfumato*[8] in drawings by Nidhal Chamekh, Massinissa Selmani and Barbara Walker, to the palimpsest drawings of Ciprian Mureşan and Lucy Skaer. What follows is an exploration of drawing as thinking through material encounter.

I begin with an examination of works by David Haines which utilise a level of mimesis and finish deemed obsolete in avant-garde circles of the early 1970s. *Your Fluffer* (2017, p.51) is a large work made with pencil on Fabriano, a hot-pressed watercolour paper which enables the artist to achieve the exact type of shading he seeks. A larger than life male figure, apparently in a state of ecstasy, rises above an assemblage of paint cans, computer screens and cables. The figure is taken from a live camera and is rendered using a matrix of graphite dots. Up close definition is lost, and at a distance a figure emerges. The lower section of the picture references the genre of still life in its traditional role of showcasing the skill and virtuosity of the artist. It is rendered with hyperrealism, a means to articulate folds in the patterned fabric and reflections on the computer screens and other polished surfaces. Yet the screens are blank, the coiled wires are like entrails in their profusion, and the paint spills like blood from a wound down the side of the tins. Rendered monochromatically, this collection of technological artefacts is abject in its excesses, hinting at impending entropy. Haines is interested in how online chat rooms change the way that humans relate to one another and his project explores the recuperative capacity of drawing to describe human emotion. The contrasting drawing modes – hyperrealist and dot matrix – remind us of the artist's touch and this drawing inhabits both categories of sign – icon and index – simultaneously.

Haines seeks to represent repressed and illicit strands of contemporary society; *My Fluffer* explores virtual interaction, while his 'Still Life with Flyer' series investigates the physical evidence of live interaction. The artist collects flyers and tickets for fringe events – folded, placed in pockets and 'body-worn' with sweat and scuffs, this paper ephemera displays traces of human use. Haines is interested in the way that the indexical marks on the flyers

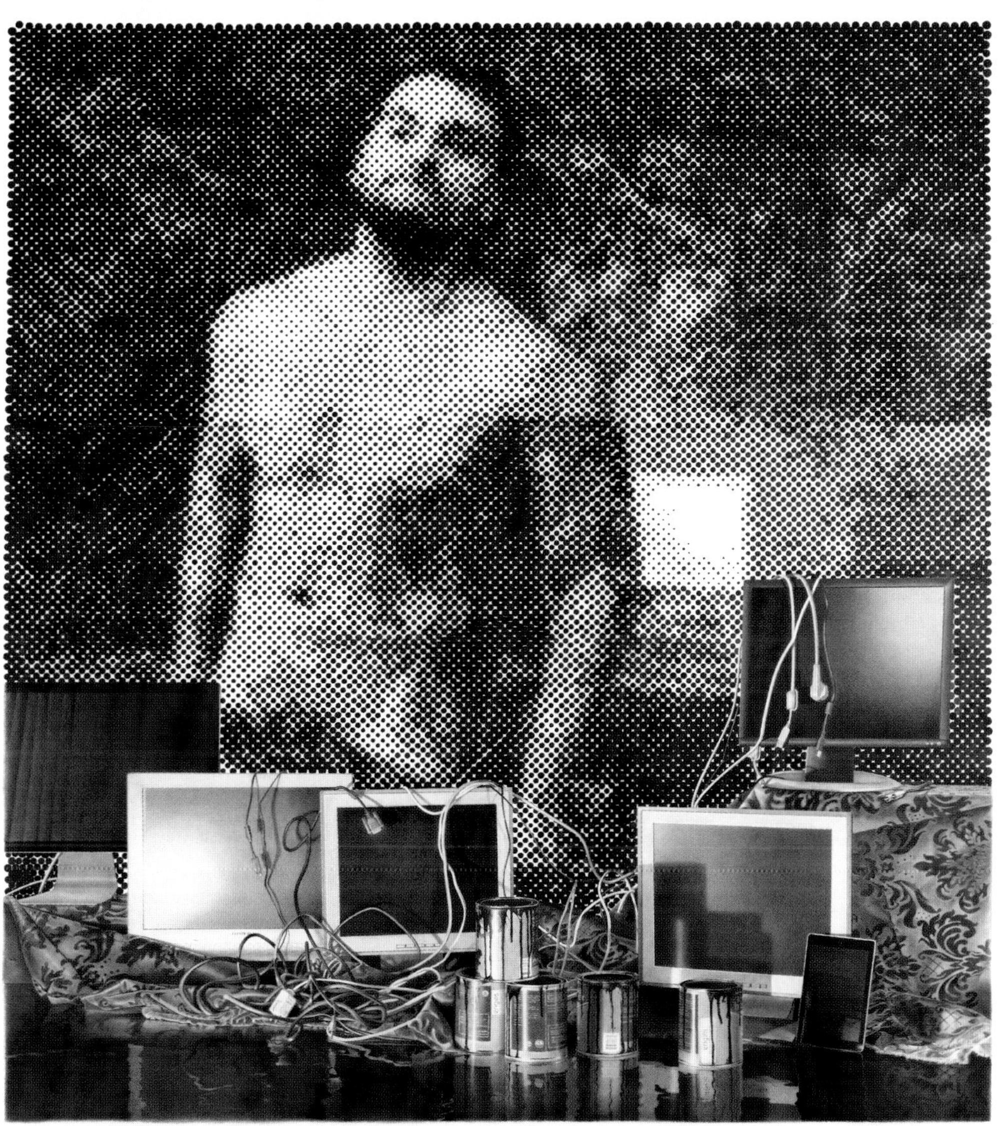

David Haines
Your Fluffer, 2017
Pencil on paper, 205 × 184 cm

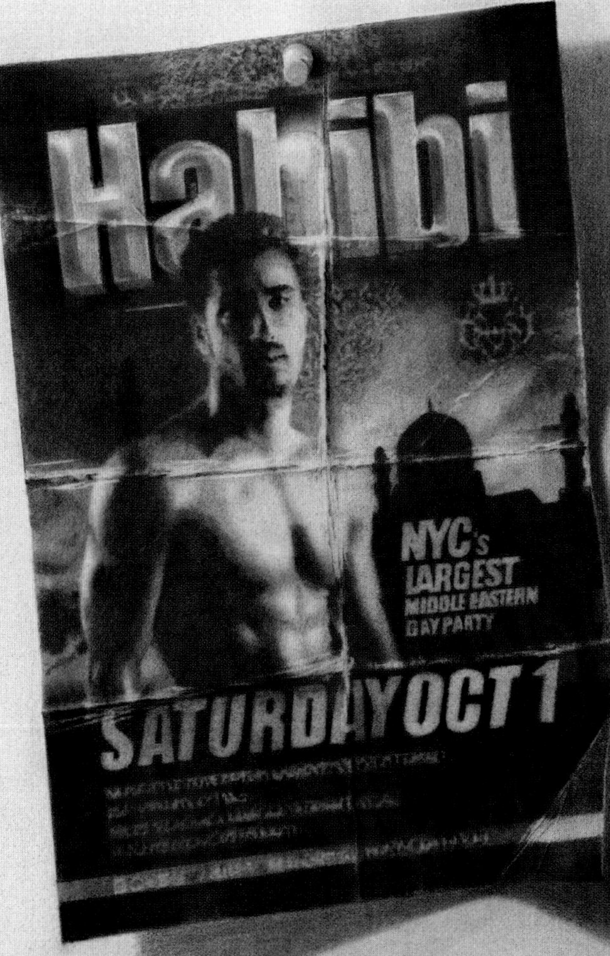
Habibi
NYC's
LARGEST
MIDDLE EASTERN
GAY PARTY
SATURDAY OCT 1

bear a direct relationship with drawing. To make exact renderings, Haines has employed trompe l'oeil, a self-reflexive technique that historically has played a role in the depiction of paper ephemera, thereby preserving peripheral moments of cultural and social history.[9] These modestly scaled works signify temporality as they engender explicit evidence of presence – of actual contact between people in a social setting, and between a person and the drawn material.

The practice of Kate Davis questions how to bear witness to the complexities of the past, and often involves responding to the aesthetic and political ambiguities of historical artworks and their reception: 'I'm drawn to art historical works that are so well known that you stop wondering about them and you turn against their work – I use drawing to question my relationship with works that have become generic and iconic through over-familiarity.'[10] Davis has used graphite in the service of photorealism in a number of projects, such as *Reversibility (It is the body and Excised)* (2011), which aimed, in Foucault's terms, to put images into circulation, in this case the photographs of Jo Spence. She chose photorealism and a high level of finish, feeling 'the need for a slow, drawn out process of engagement with her images as I wanted the resulting drawings to communicate a high level of investment from me in her work – a respect – paying homage.'[11] Yet Davis struggles with the mechanical way in which

a photorealist mode of drawing treats the maker as a tool, like a camera, and erases any subjective expression or trace of the author, the maker. She employed a purely indexical form of drawing in *Disgrace* to liberate herself from such constraints. *Disgrace* (2009, pp.4, 54–55) is a series of drawings and a video that examine Davis's relationship with the Italian artist Amedeo Modigliani. Like most of us, she learnt about Modigliani's nudes through photographic reproductions; indeed, she grew up with one on her living room wall. She found herself seduced by the sinuous lines he used to describe the female form, yet repelled by his representation of women as vacuous, empty shells: 'Prior to making the *Disgrace* series I had been working on several labour-intensive photorealist drawings and I was trying to challenge myself to make some drawings which were much more immediate and I was less in control.'[12] To make *Disgrace* Davis lay on black and white reproductions of Modigliani's nudes, and drew around her body, mapping as much of it as possible onto the page, superimposing her graphite lines over his: 'For me, the drawing began to do something interesting when the bodies 'mingled' or there was a kind of breakdown between them and it became difficult to discern where either body started or ended.'[13] Davis's drawn lines track her body as a living, breathing being, rather than as image.

Karl Haendel makes drawings, paintings, artist books and videos and like Davis[14] employs

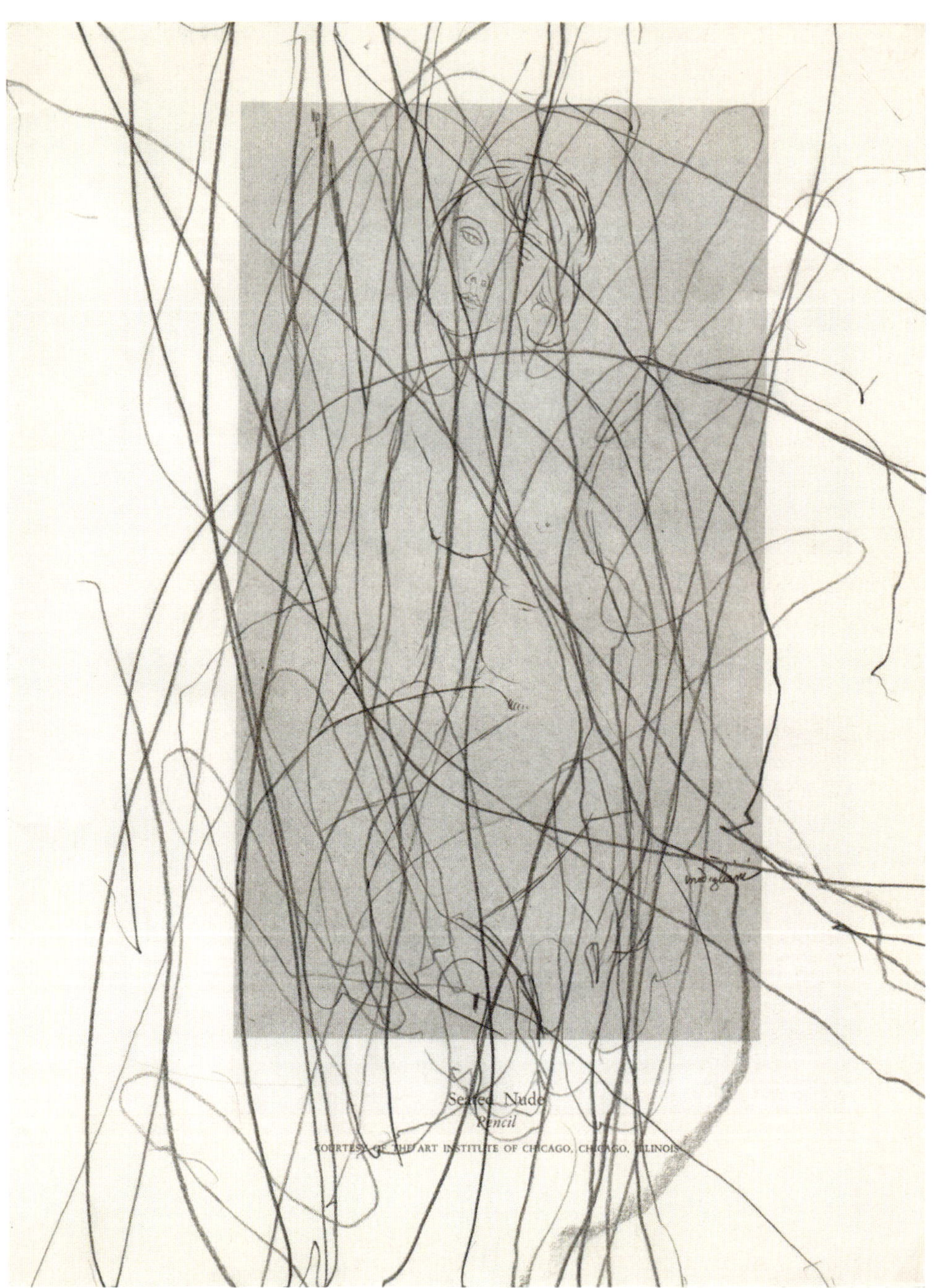

Kate Davis

Disgrace I, 2009

Pencil on page from monograph, 44 × 35 cm

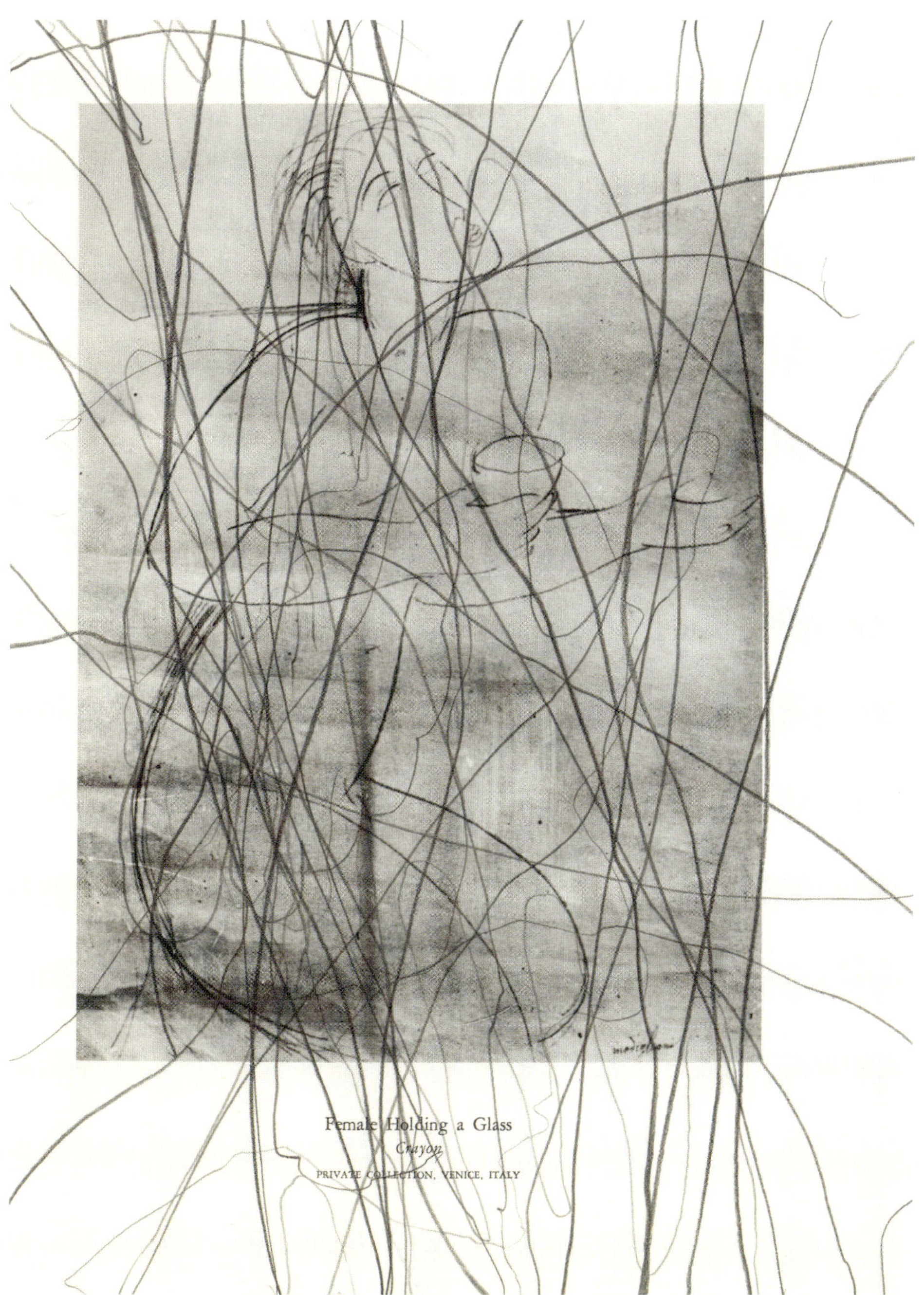

Kate Davis
Disgrace IV, 2009
Pencil on page from monograph, 44 × 35 cm

structures which the viewer is forced to navigate in order to access his drawings. *Weeks in Wet Sheets* (2015, pp.57–60) is an installation consisting of 30 drawings, which for the present exhibition is split across both venues. This work takes water as its subject, and investigates our political, social, environmental and linguistic understanding of wetness as a concept. The drawings vary in scale and are generally unframed, displayed amid and upon cardboard plinths and sections of painted wall. The arrangement appears ad hoc, rather like a trade fair stand. It could be the physical manifestation of a virtual confection, empty of any markers of reality.

Haendel has said: 'My drawings are about the real world. What *is* unstable in my work is their metaphorical possibilities.'[15] Each image in *Weeks in Wet Sheets* has been carefully selected to represent a type, or category; Haendel is suggesting that these iconic images are as innately neutral as words, and like them only gain meaning in context. Haendel employs a classification system to file images, and upon retrieval these are projected onto a grid, to ensure the drawing's fidelity to its source. Nonetheless, the 30 drawings comprising *Weeks in Wet Sheets* constitute a constellation of drawing modes. Like Davis[16], Haendel uses stock images, such as that of a yacht; or wine, cheese and grapes to represent the Californian city of Salinas, known as the 'salad bowl of the world.' These are drawn using hard graphite, delicate shading to render

shallow pictorial space, and are occasionally framed, conferring upon them the status of 'picture'. Animals that depend on water and are now at risk by climate change, such as the hippo, the toad, and the beaver, are cut-outs, sensitively rendered in soft graphite, and teetering perilously upon towers of ill-fitting geometric shapes. In some drawings the hand of the artist can be detected in the pencil strokes, such as *Fixtures* – sanitary fittings in a strangely atmospheric and beguiling setting. The labour-intensive drawings contradict the artificiality and transitory nature of the display and remind us of the dichotomy of the human condition: vulnerable yet destructive, selfish yet dependent on each other and increasingly abstract systems.

Haendel employs a number of strategies to attend to paper as physical entity. The most obvious is his use of the edge of the paper; in many instances graphite deposits cover each fibre of a roughly torn edge. He also cuts into sheets of paper to produce geometric shapes, and voids, or blank areas of paper, to disrupt a one-dimensional view onto the world, to investigate '… how lines can be themselves and in service of representation.'[17]

Nidhal Chamekh also works from found images, but selects those relating to concerns shaped by his personal experience of Tunisian political turmoil, both historical and contemporary. In *Trois Poses de Fadhel Sassi (Three Poses of Fadhel Sassi)* (2016, pp.62–63),

opposite and following spread
Karl Haendel
Weeks in Wet Sheets, 2015
Works on paper and cardboard elements, installation view

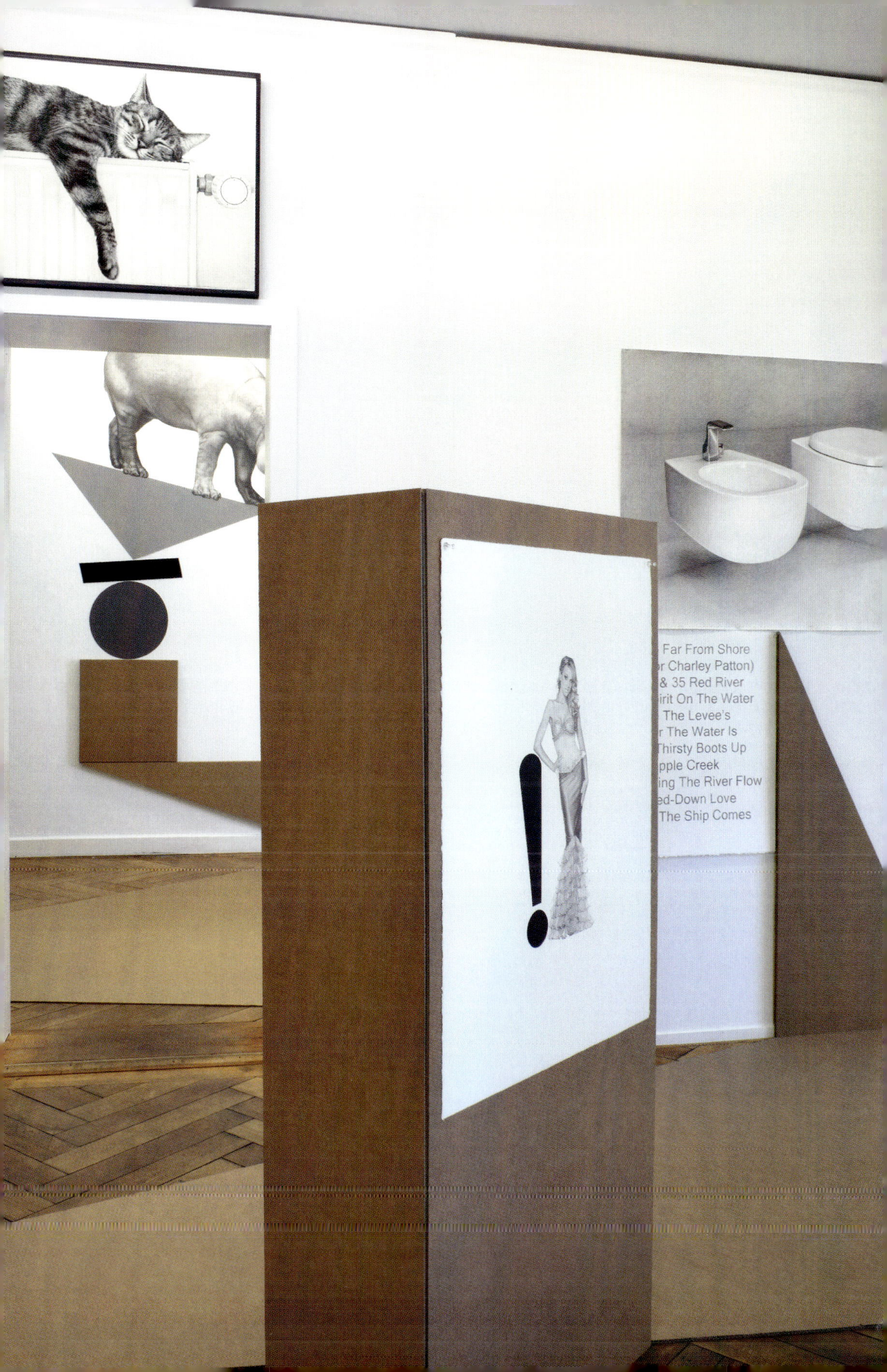
Far From Shore
or Charley Patton)
& 35 Red River
irit On The Water
The Levee's
r The Water Is
Thirsty Boots Up
pple Creek
ing The River Flow
ed-Down Love
The Ship Comes

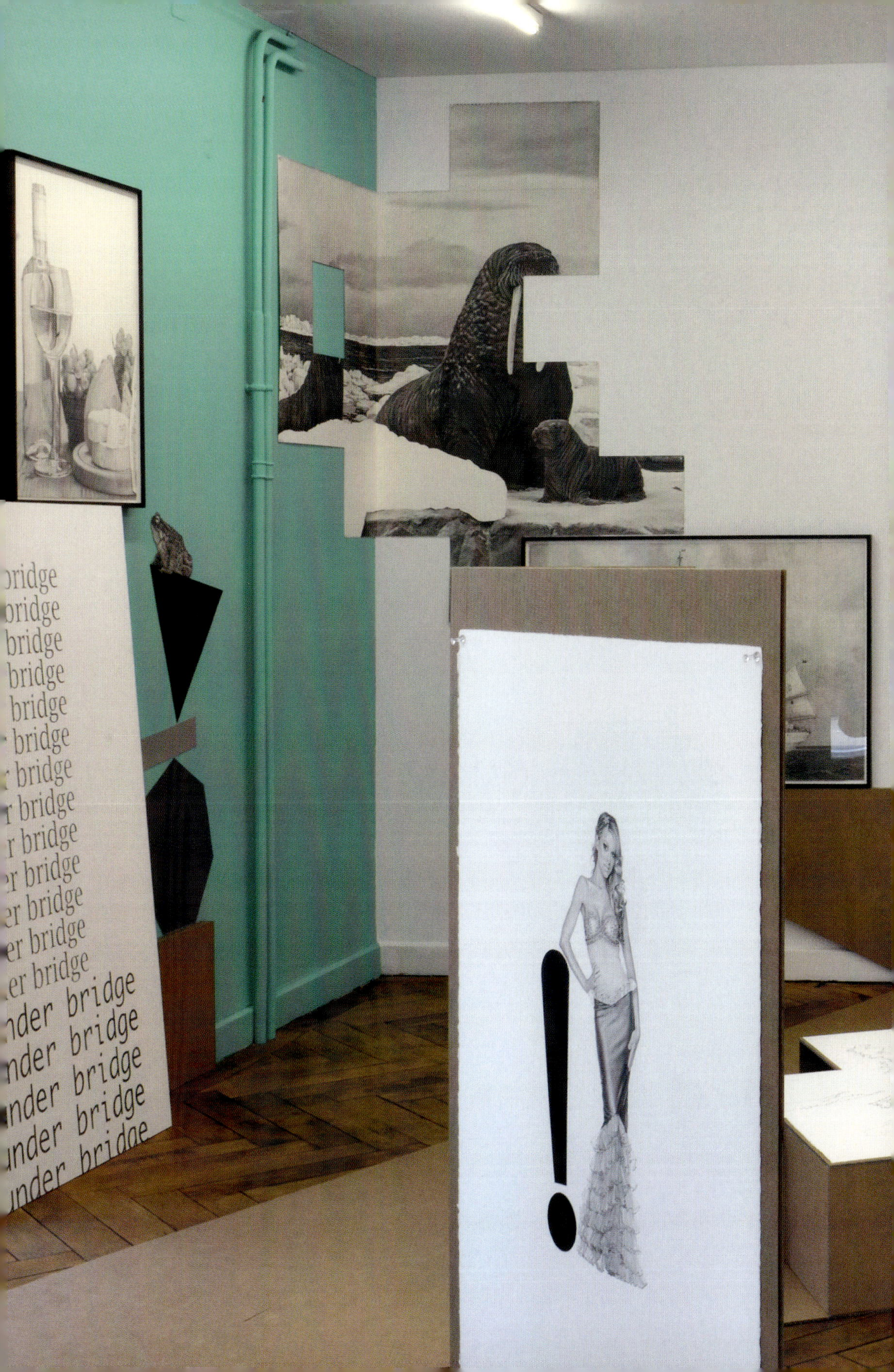
bridge
bridge
bridge
bridge
bridge
bridge
r bridge
er bridge
er bridge
nder bridge
nder bridge
nder bridge
nder bridge
under bridge

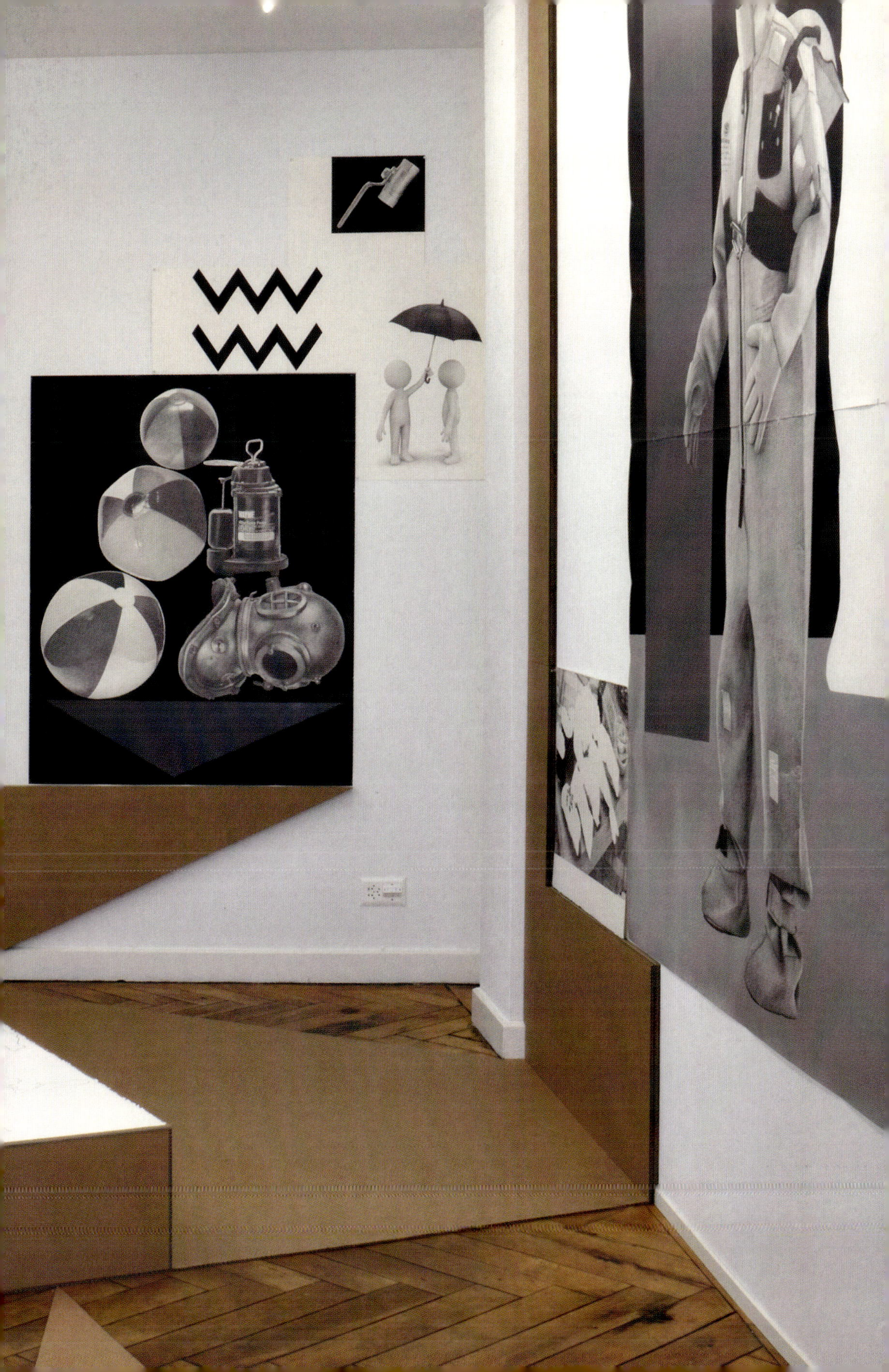

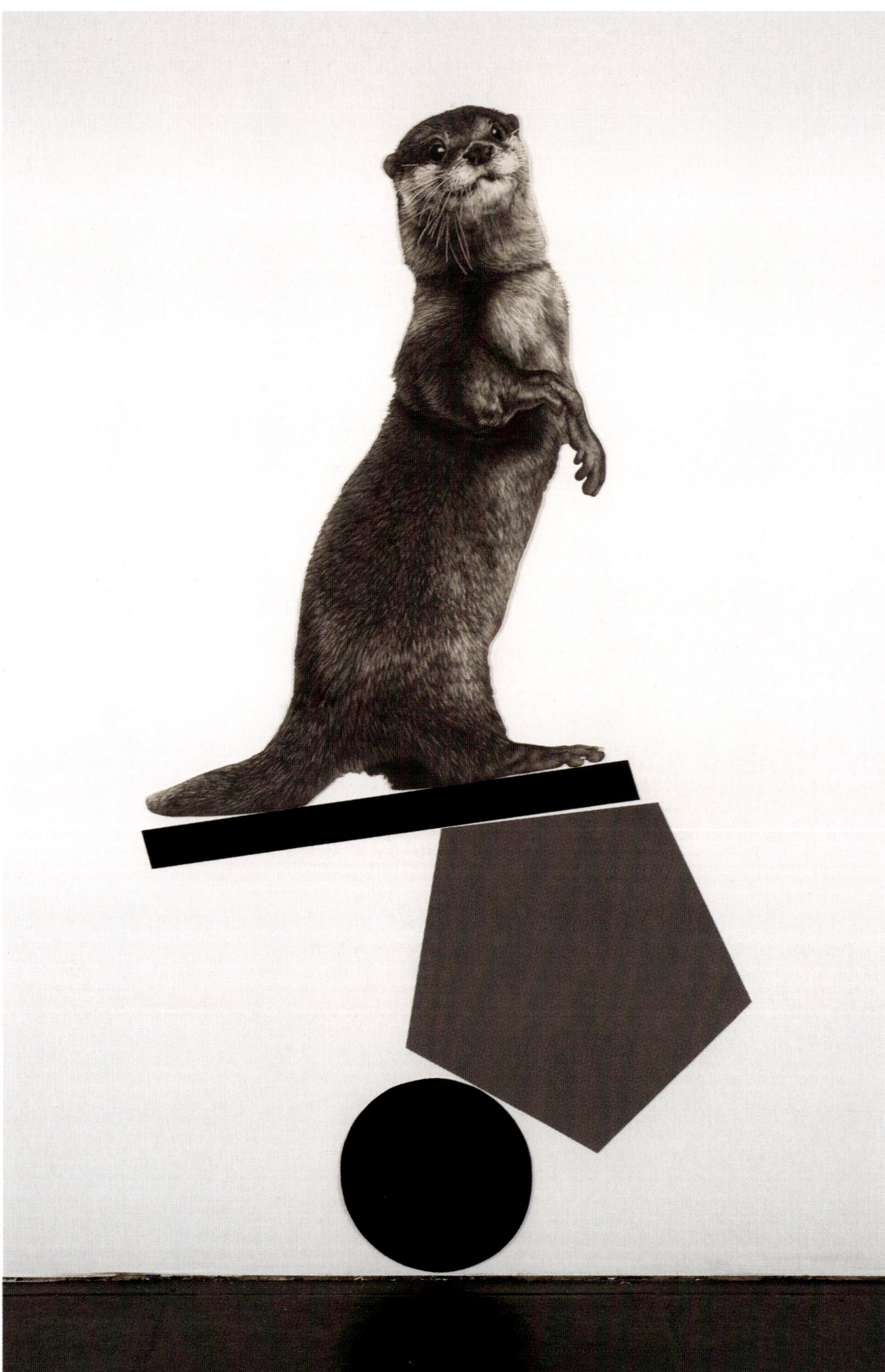

Chamekh tackles the large-scale format of the history painting, using classical composition and proportion to relate, across three panels, the narrative of a dying man. The title identifies the subject as Fadhel Sassi, who was a teacher, poet and an activist in the Tunisian Democratic Patriots' Movement. On 3 January 1984 he was shot by government forces in downtown Tunis, during a demonstration against bread shortages. Fadhel Sassi had been a colleague of the artist's mother and Chamekh found the source newspaper cutting in the family archive. He wanted to put this hidden image of the victim of state-sponsored violence back into circulation. The titular 'Three Poses' makes clear that his act is not one of mimesis; Chamekh altered the orientation of the original image to inject the composition with movement and drama, further increased through his use of *pentimenti*. The artist typically makes his own charcoal, in this instance from burnt bread, to render marks of varying intensity and precision in the production of images that reveal as much as they hide. Blank areas of canvas are used to dramatic effect, and the spreading pool of blood on the drain cover leaps to the surface as an abstract element of the composition.

Barbara Walker, like Chamekh, selects images that provide evidence of discriminatory regimes. She is particularly drawn to those that tackle historic and contemporary cultural difference, and her drawings memorialise overlooked individuals and groups. An intensive six-year project has led Walker to the archives of the Imperial War Museum, the National Army Museum and online archival services including the Jamaican Library, researching the records of black servicemen and women. The resulting works reflect upon the contributions of the British West Indies Regiment and the King's African Rifles, among others, and address gender and the under-recognised role of servicewomen from the Caribbean and West India Regiments in World War II. Walker chooses drawing as a labour intensive yet reversible process that facilitates acts of retrieval, restoration, and recuperation.

Walker has a growing collection of vintage portrait images, their subjects largely anonymous, such as that used as the source of a large, untitled portrait made directly onto the wall (2017, p.66). Here she used conté and pastel to render the anxious and vulnerable black soldier, making explicit the hand of the artist: 'you can see where I've been, what I've done. It's only charcoal.'[18] Walker transports this forgotten and overlooked individual to the status of hero through the large scale of the drawing (over two metres high) and a red background, a colour long associated with royalty and power, and in the 20th century with uprising and revolution. Fragments of pastel and conté stain the gallery floor, a residue of her labours and a metaphor for the soldier's spilled blood. Having toiled to render this young soldier's face with the utmost attention to detail, Walker erased the modelled forms with a wet rag to produce dirty smears that

61

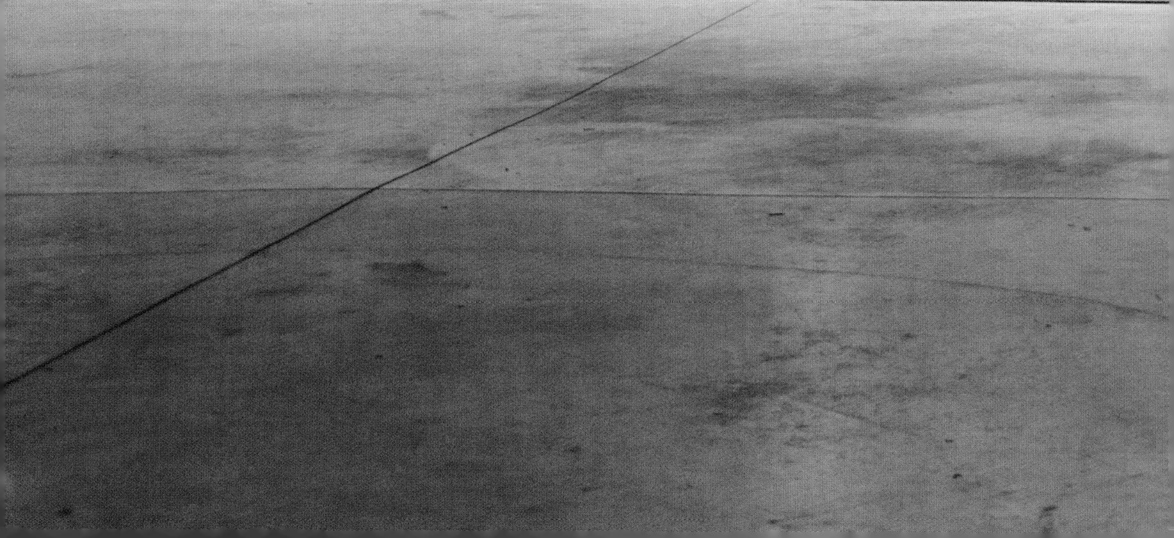

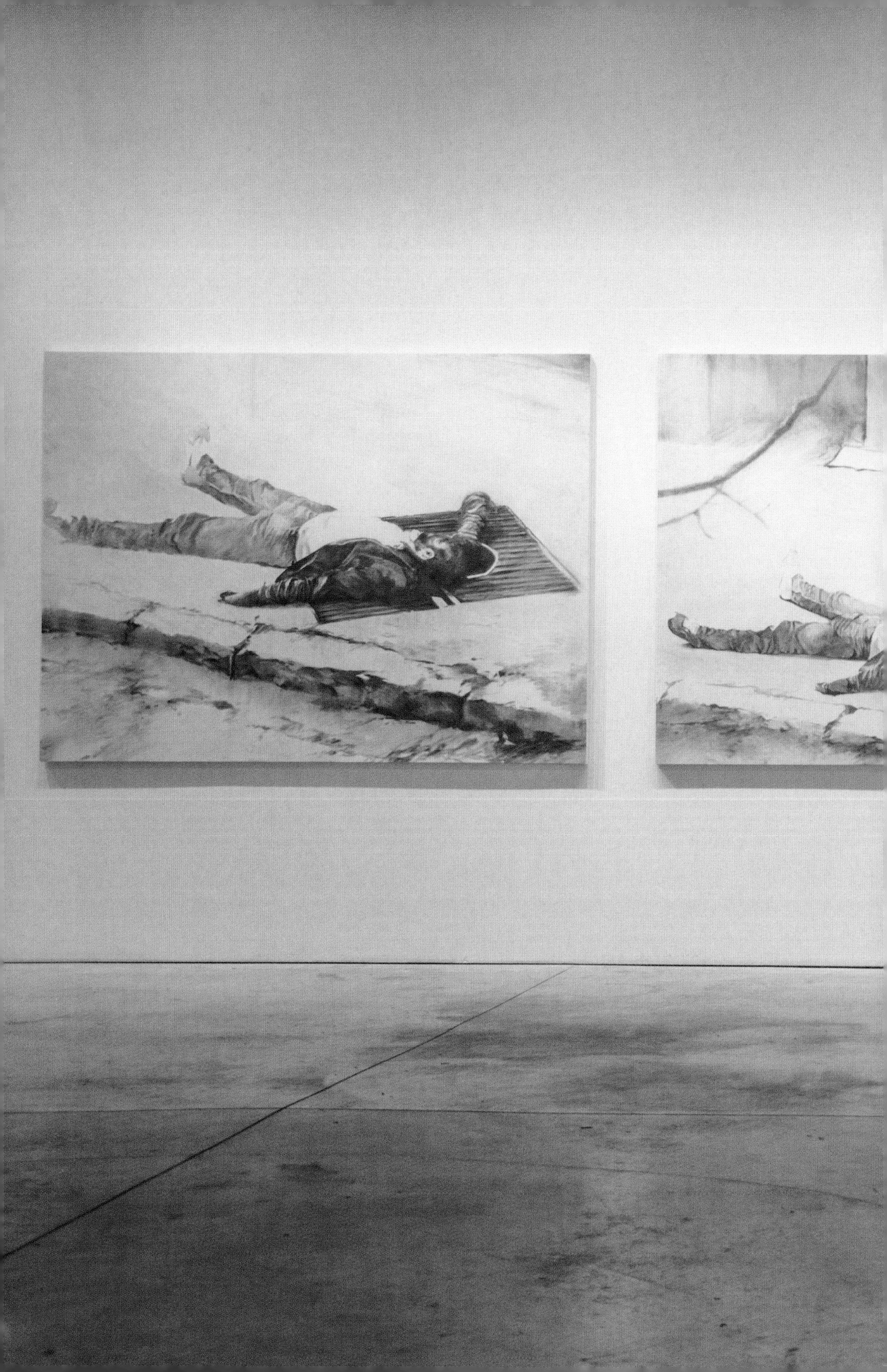

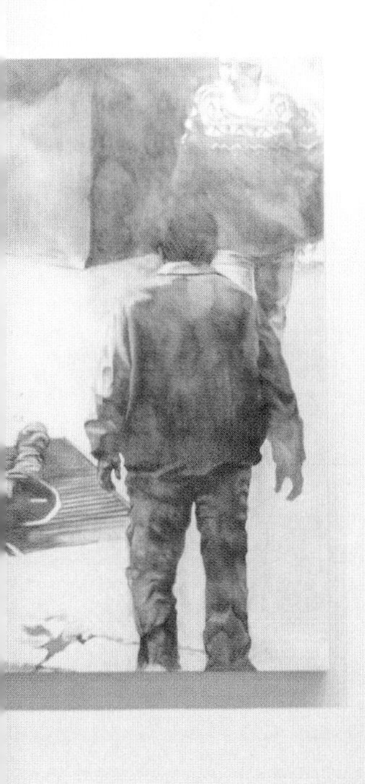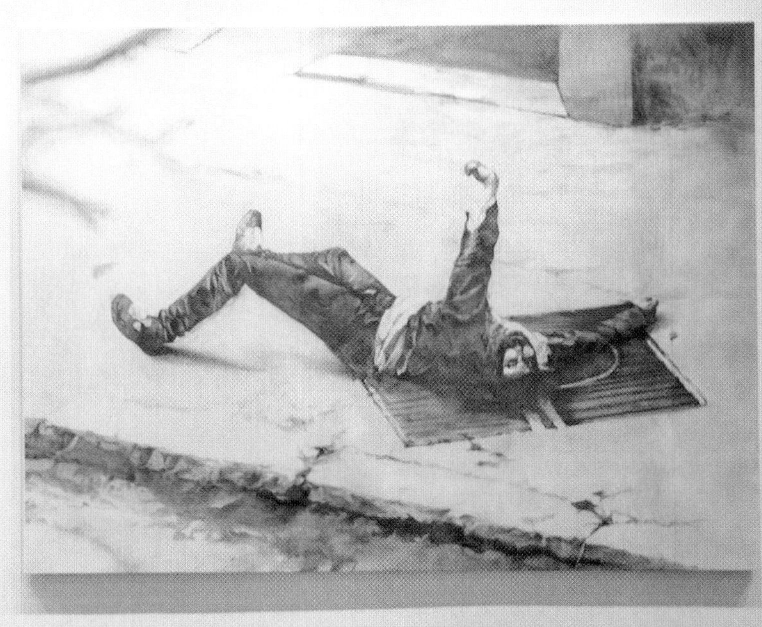

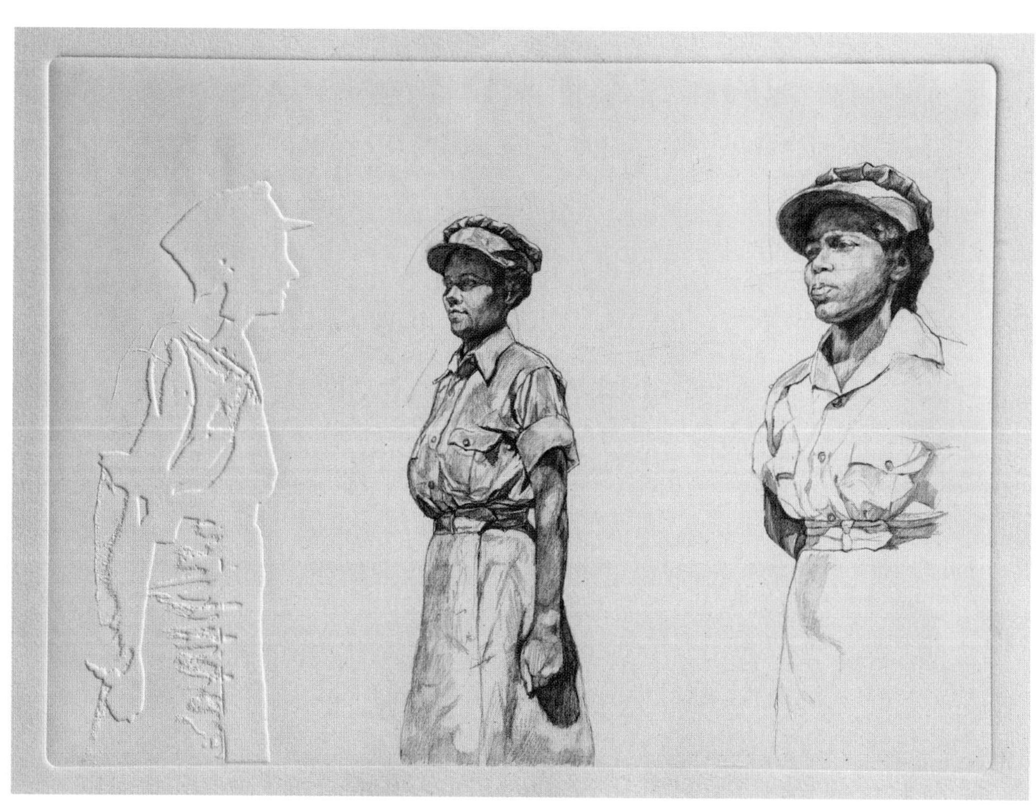

Barbara Walker
Parade III, 2017
Graphite on embossed paper, 51 × 61 cm

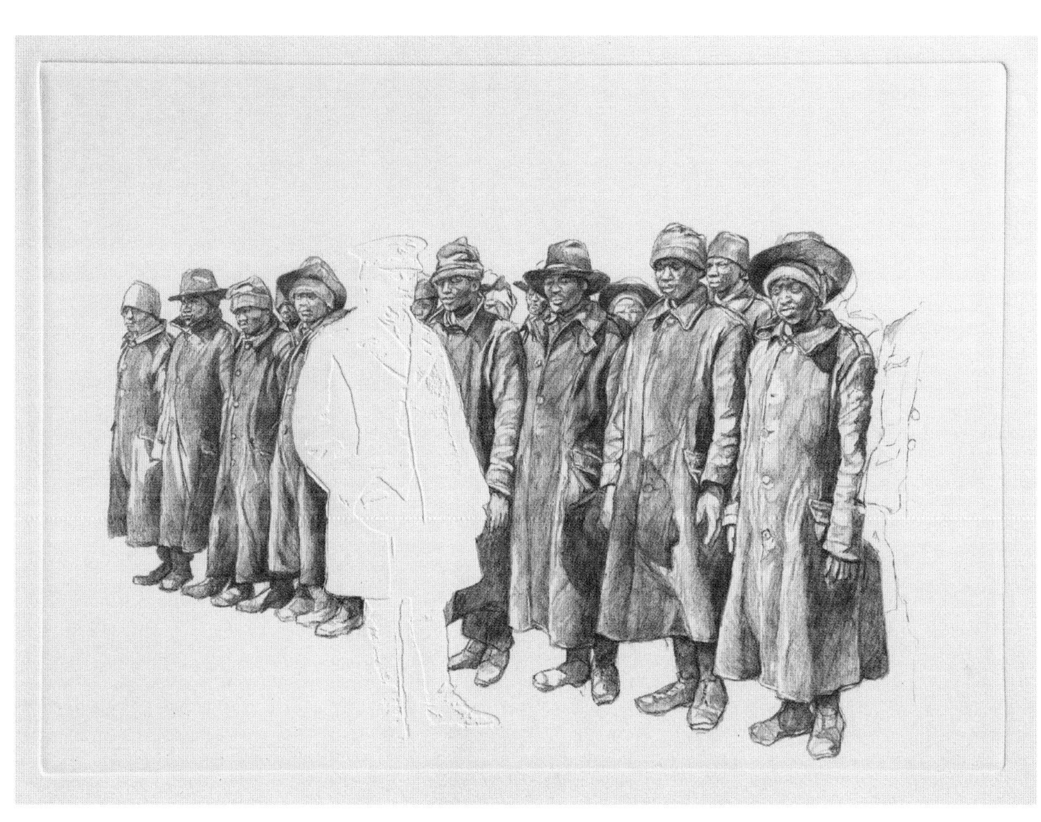

Barbara Walker
Parade II, 2017
Graphite on embossed paper, 51 × 61 cm

18/04 /1918

threaten the integrity of her figuration. This is one of a number of strategies that Walker has employed to explore ways to visualise the invisibility or lack of representation and recognition of black army personnel.

Parade II (2017, p.65) is one of a new series of small-scale works in which Walker experiments with embossing to mark absence. She has edited the found image, erasing the background to leave her drawn figures anchorless, stranded on the expanse of white paper – hovering, barely there. She has rendered in graphite a parade of black men, their coats ill-fitting, feet irregular in worn shoes, heads hanging in subjugation and bearing assorted and tatty hats, hand-me-downs rather than military issue clothing. In her tender rendering and attention to detail Walker seems to be atoning for the mistreatment of these men. In contradistinction, no material traces delineate the commanding officer who is visualised through embossing, a mechanical process which produces lines in relief. This clinical procedure captures the crisp, well-fitting uniform and clipped demeanour, and has a dehumanising effect.

David Musgrave employs drawing, painting, animation and writing to explore the human experience in a world increasingly determined by abstract digital systems. He creates images that exist at the periphery of recognition, that oscillate between familiarity and the unknown, tapping into our capacity to identify the human figure in a seemingly random and accidental assemblage of marks and traces.

Musgrave investigates how the ancient technology of drawing can be repurposed to echo generative and plastic digital processes. He begins with a sliver of material that has psychological resonance – either an object that he finds or a rough maquette that he fashions in the studio. The translation of this trigger image into a drawing is not an act of mimesis, it is rather one of inventing as he goes along, each mark laid down determining the scope of his project, pushing to the extreme the expressive limits of graphite, a compressed form of matter.

Musgrave's graphite drawings continue the long artistic tradition of self-consciously employing trompe l'oeil to render paper ephemera. He uses this technique to create an illusion, but the uncertain status of the image draws attention to the methodology of production. For example, *Large plane* (2006, p.70) is an even graphite ground, the lines that form the stick figure appearing as scratches into a soft, skin-like surface. The drawn crease in the grey board bisects the entire pictorial field, and scars the pulpy surface, whilst the artist has tenderly depicted scraps of tape, notional sticking plasters, at seemingly random points. Together these details obliterate any distinction between the ground of the drawing and graphic representation. *Plane with paper scraps* (2006, p.71)

Barbara Walker
Out of the Dark, 2017, Drawing Room Bursary Award
Conté and pastel on wall, 250 × 117 cm

is more obviously contrived, the legibility of the figure challenged by the diffuse scattering of torn paper. In *Spirit plane no. 3* (2015, p.69) no drawn lines are visible, and yet we comprehend folds and creases that coalesce into a rudimentary anthropomorphic form. Through the most minimal shading, created with a very hard pencil, Musgrave conveys the impression of a piece of paper that has been folded and then straightened out. A narrow border confirms the artifice of the image. In each of these drawings the graphite is built invisibly, and is barely there, as if airbrushed onto the paper. Musgrave has said: 'I'm not trying to represent things but embody them, be them.'[19] He wishes to engender an encounter with both base materials and with memory and recognition, to trigger a psychological response.

Massinissa Selmani also pursues an interest in conjuring surreal imagery to induce a sense of the uncanny, but his articulation stands in contrast to Musgrave's inflection-free drawing. Selmani employs cross-hatched lines to produce figures engaged in curious acts, variously benign, malicious and downright strange, with drop shadows evoking a shallow sense of space. His characters and props relate to the corrupt behaviour of politicians and the media, both today and in the recent past. Invariably modest in scale, and often transgressing the parameters of the paper edge, Selmani adopts different drawing modes to suit the needs of each project. Frequently taking an archival approach, he makes many sketchy unframed

drawings that incorporate collage and tracing paper layers. He also creates finished, carefully conceived compositions, such as *Récit d'Arrangements (A Tale of Arrangements)* (2017, pp.72, 73). As with many of his drawings, characters are extracted from different press clippings and combined to create unlikely situations: 'The idea is to avoid the context and create a new one, between reality and fiction'.[20] Selmani produces the image using short, broken strokes of the pencil to create volume, a form of *sfumato*. Selmani's pencil strokes possess a graphic energy which conveys a sense of urgency. In *Récit d'Arrangements No. III* (p.73) four men with solemn expressions carry a sock upon a flat board; to their right, a man stands at a podium, looking down at his notes and directing the viewer's gaze towards his stockinged and unshod feet. A fantastical transplantation has occurred: the upright sock, with bright blue stripes, which burdens the 'pall bearers' is surely a metaphor for a dead body; that the orator also wears stripy socks, albeit monochromatic, suggests that he is in fact no longer of this world.

There is a delicate interplay between the iconic and the indexical in Selmani's drawings; they are unassuming yet engender, albeit quite differently, the 'minor material violence' that Musgrave seeks to convey. As the title *Récit d'Arrangements* indicates, these are choreographed scenes in which a number of characters negotiate positions of power, subjugation, deviance and conformity; the

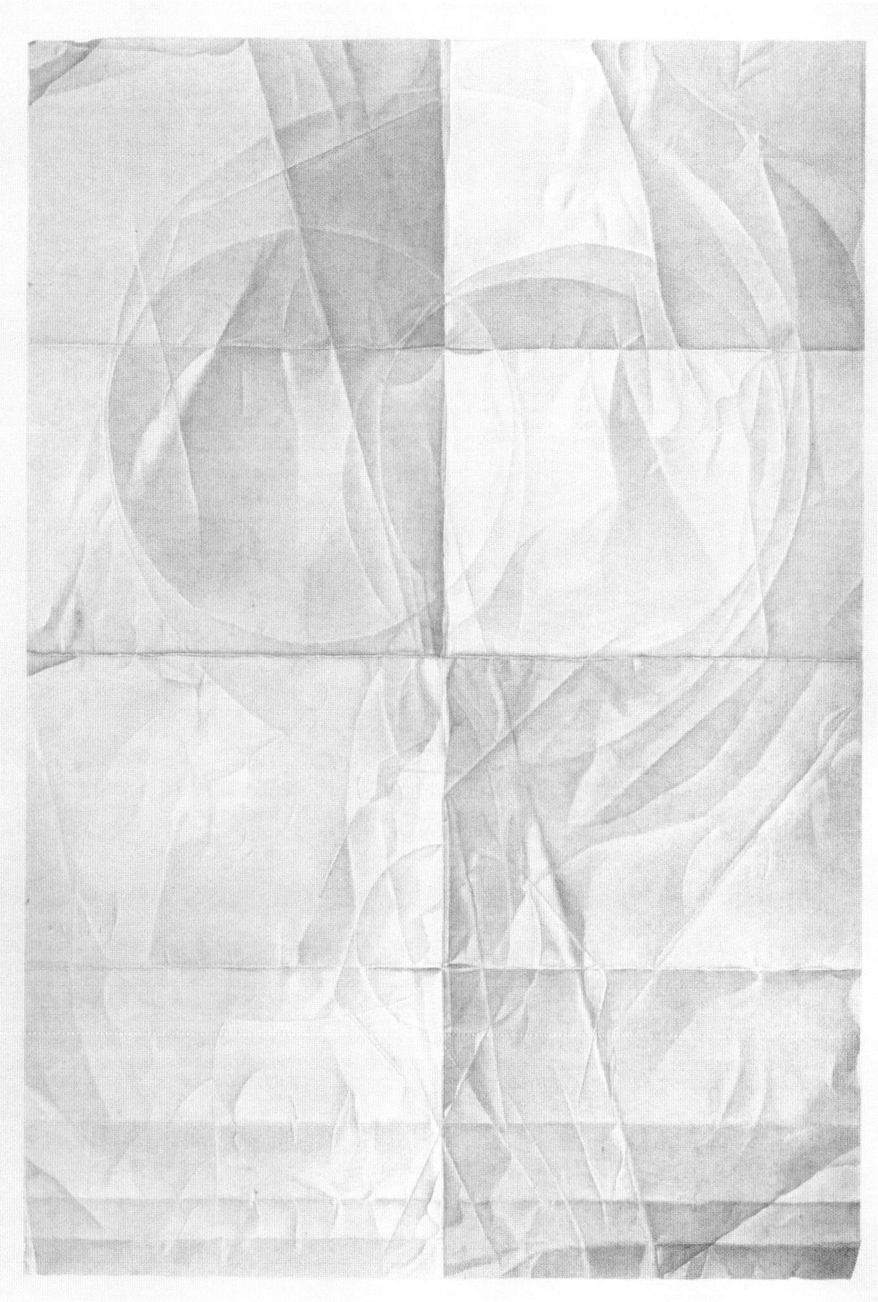

David Musgrave
Spirit plane no.3, 2015
Graphite on paper, 104.8 × 74.4 cm

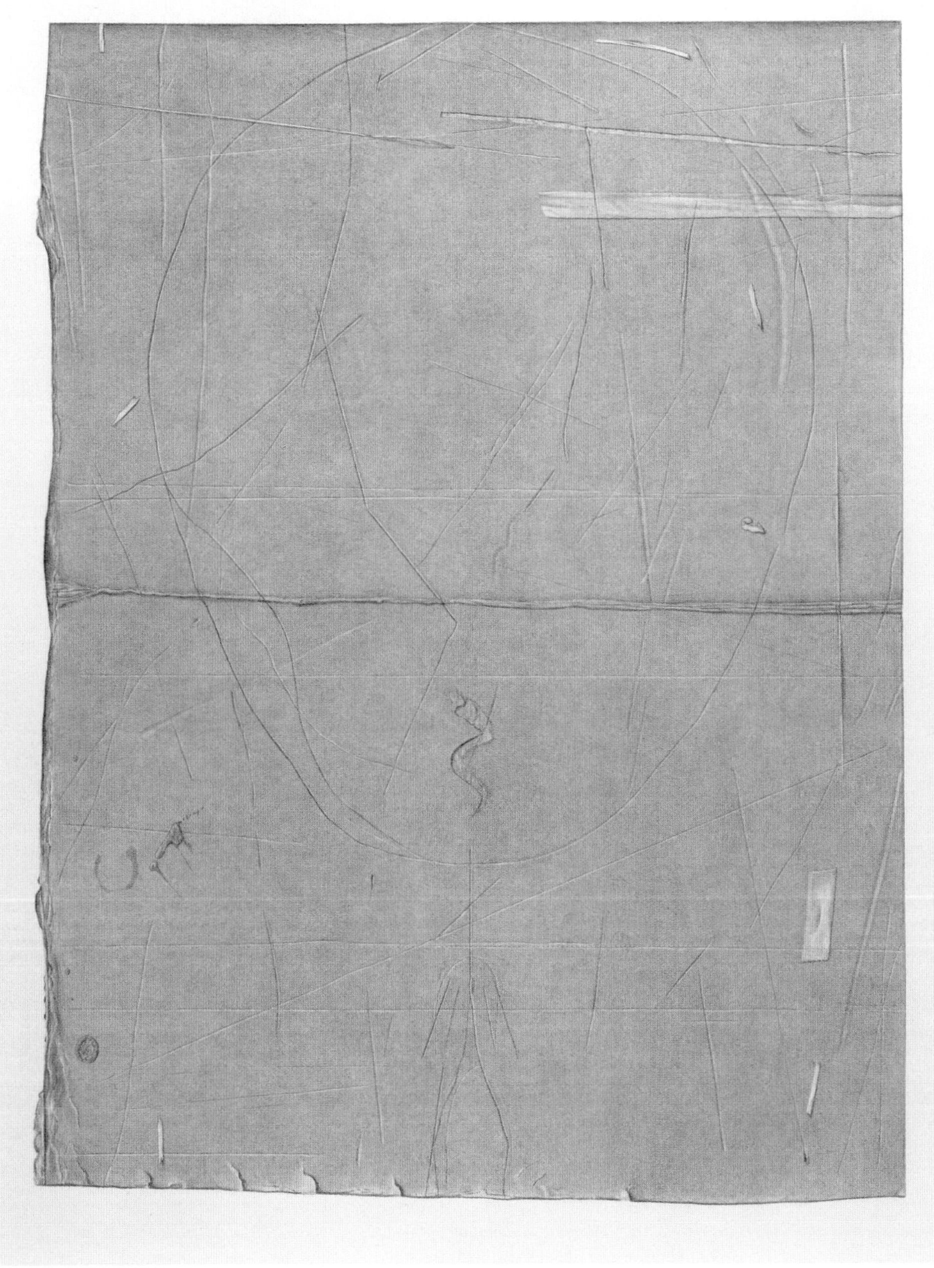

David Musgrave
Large plane, 2006
Graphite on paper, 66.2 × 51 cm

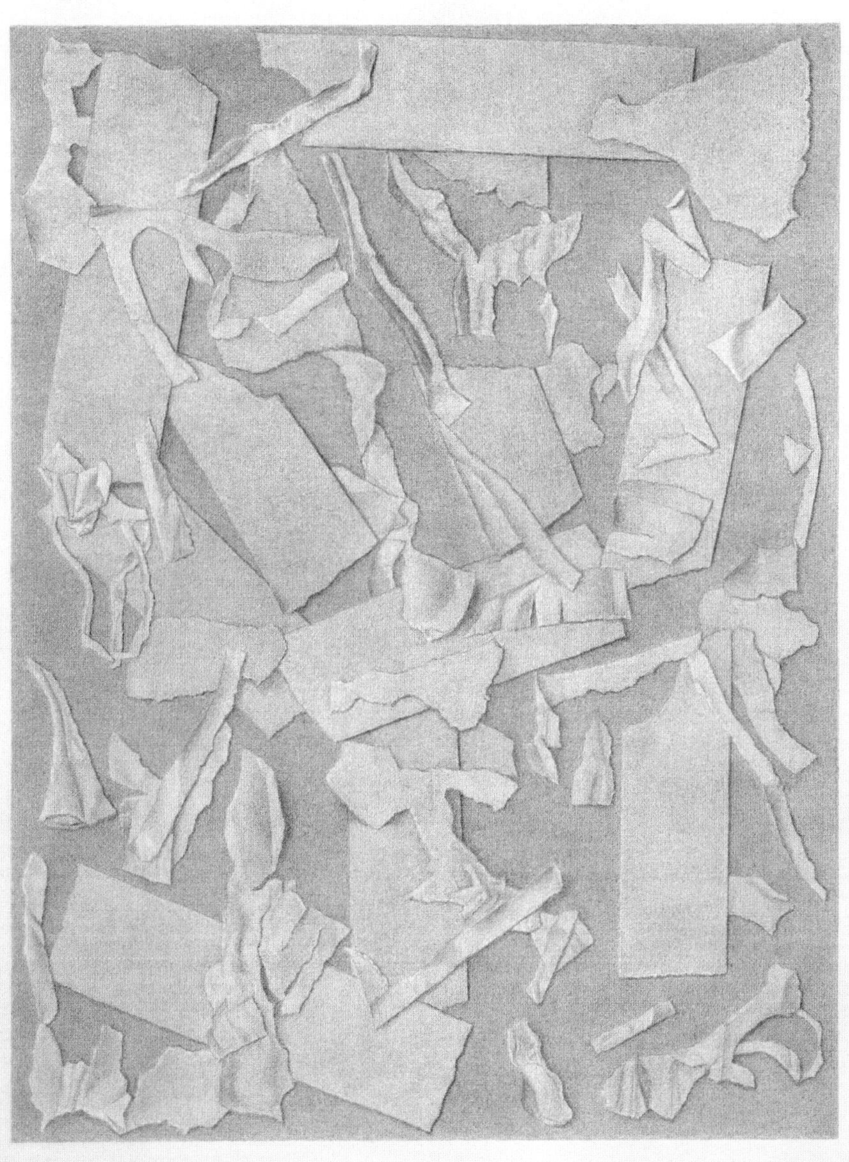

David Musgrave

Plane with paper scraps, 2006

Graphite on paper, 47.6 × 37.8 cm

Massinissa Selmani
Récit d'Arrangements No.1, 2017
Graphite and coloured pencil on paper, 42 × 52 cm

Massınıssa Selmanı
Récit d'Arrangements No. III, 2017
Graphite and coloured pencil on paper, 42 × 52 cm

vignettes conjure sensations of menace, benevolence, violence and cooperation, all through the subtle handling of sensitive, cross-hatched lines. Like Haendel, Selmani employs formal tricks, using blank areas of the paper to remind us of its insubstantial means, whilst the graphite and coloured pencil marks hover between icon and index.

In a pre-photographic era skilled draughtsmen toiled to translate artworks into reproducible engravings, and the hand of the individual craftsman was celebrated. Today we learn about art history through photographic reproductions, an invisible lens that brings the original artwork to our attention. In 1930 the art historian Erwin Panofsky observed that photographs conveyed facture (the texture and physical qualities of artworks created through the manipulation of graphite or paint) in a way that earlier forms of reproduction did not.[21] He noted that black and white photographs, in particular, reinforced a modern way of seeing art by drawing attention to the mark making and texture.

It is interesting to consider these observations in light of the prolific and substantial drawing practice of Ciprian Mureşan, who grew up in communist Romania and had little access to original works of art. His drawing oeuvre responds to the ramifications of political regimes on today's global politics through the prism of his personal experience of learning about art history, almost exclusively, through reproduction.

The inspiration for Mureşan's palimpsest drawings was the myth that the Dutch artist Bas Jan Ader drew on the same piece of paper for four years, erasing one drawing before beginning the next. *All Images from a Book on Bas Jan Ader* (2013) was the first in the palimpsest series – pencil drawings that record every illustration in an art book, journal or exhibition catalogue through a technique of superimposing one image over the next. Other works in the series include *All Images from a Book on Agnes Martin* (2014), and *All Images from a Book on Matthias Grünewald* (2014). Each illustration is drawn onto a large sheet of paper (the source publication determines the format of the composition) starting at top left, and line by line forms a grid of images. When Mureşan reaches the end of the sheet he goes back to the start, working on top of the earlier drawings to continue his exercise. Even as the drawings approach a blackened miasma we can recognise the unmistakable cool, detached lines of Agnes Martin, or the harmonious forms of Masaccio. Earlier drawings are buried, consigned to a jumble of black lines, a perfect visualisation of the way in which images become engrained, conditioning our perception of the world, as described by Mureşan:

I acknowledge that this distant, foggy pedagogy of the copy is ingrained in my take on pictures in general, which feel always predated and somehow lessoned by the previous, spectral incarnation as copies. And it might be more interesting to see how this subjective experience might correlate to how images function today, how we process contemporary visual experience, how old and new simulacra compete for attention.[22]

Palimpsest, Artforum March 2008 (2) (2016, pp.76–77) is one of a larger series in which Mureşan drew every single advertisement in successive issues of *Artforum*. This issue was published months before the global financial crash, precipitated by the collapse of US investment bank Lehman Brothers in September 2008. Mureşan's drawing is a palimpsest of the art market at the perilous height of late capitalism. Art world 'brand names' slowly emerge from the graphite miasma: museums, commercial galleries, and blue-chip artist names. Looking at the series as a whole, details move in and out of focus, legible in more fallow times and subsumed within the density of black pencil lines in bumper issues. The lines are compact and almost frantically scribbled in places, the content almost erased by the force of mark making, whilst the smudges and thumbprints around the edges draw attention to the misalignment of the magazine pages in the overlay. It is hard to imagine a better way to express materially the escalating bubble of global finance, inextricably fuelled by the capitalist consumption of art as over-performing investment, visualised by Mureşan on the eve of its almost inevitable implosion.

Mureşan's *Andrei Rublev by Tarkovsky, sec. 21–30* (2017, pp.78–79) is one of a trilogy of drawings based on Andrei Tarkovsky's film *Andrei Rublev* (1966) which was produced during the height of censorship in Russia. The subject of Tarkovsky's film is the life of the 15th century Russian monk and icon painter Andrei Rublev. Set during the Mongol invasion, a bleak and desperate time for the Russian people, the misfortunes of Rublev unfold in black and white. At the very end of the three-hour film, Rublev's icon paintings appear in full and splendid colour, a symbol of Tarkovsky's belief in art as salvation. Mureşan's palimpsest monochrome series in graphite on paper seems to question the redemptive capacity of art even whilst acknowledging the influence of Tarkovsky on his work and that of his Romanian artist peers. In *Andrei Rublev by Tarkovsky, sec. 21-30* Mureşan retains the 16:9 cinemascope ratio of the film and once again employs the palimpsest as an artistic strategy. Using drawing rather than film[23] for close observation, Mureşan sets out 48 frames, each containing rapidly discharged lines that agglomerate to form the rowing boat figure and describe how little his position changes within these 10 seconds of film. Like Tarkovsky's film, this drawing conveys stillness, the viewer comprehending Mureşan's second by second observation, such that, like Tarkovsky's films, 'not only does it live within time, but time lives within it'.[24] Mureşan's drawings encapsulate the time of making the drawing, or watching a film, or

following spread
Ciprian Mureşan
Palimpsest, Artforum March 2008 (2), 2016
Pencil on paper, 152 × 209 cm

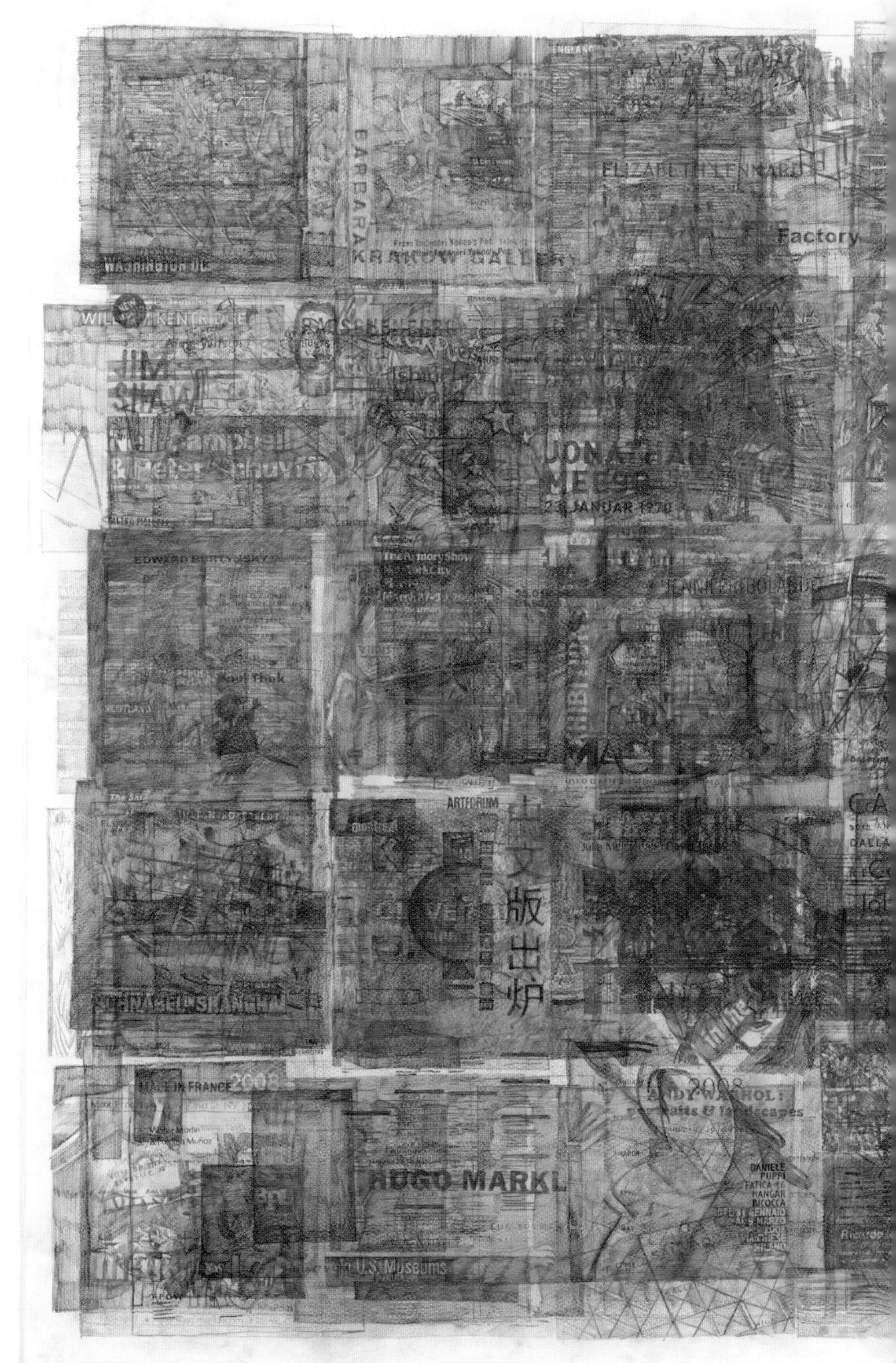

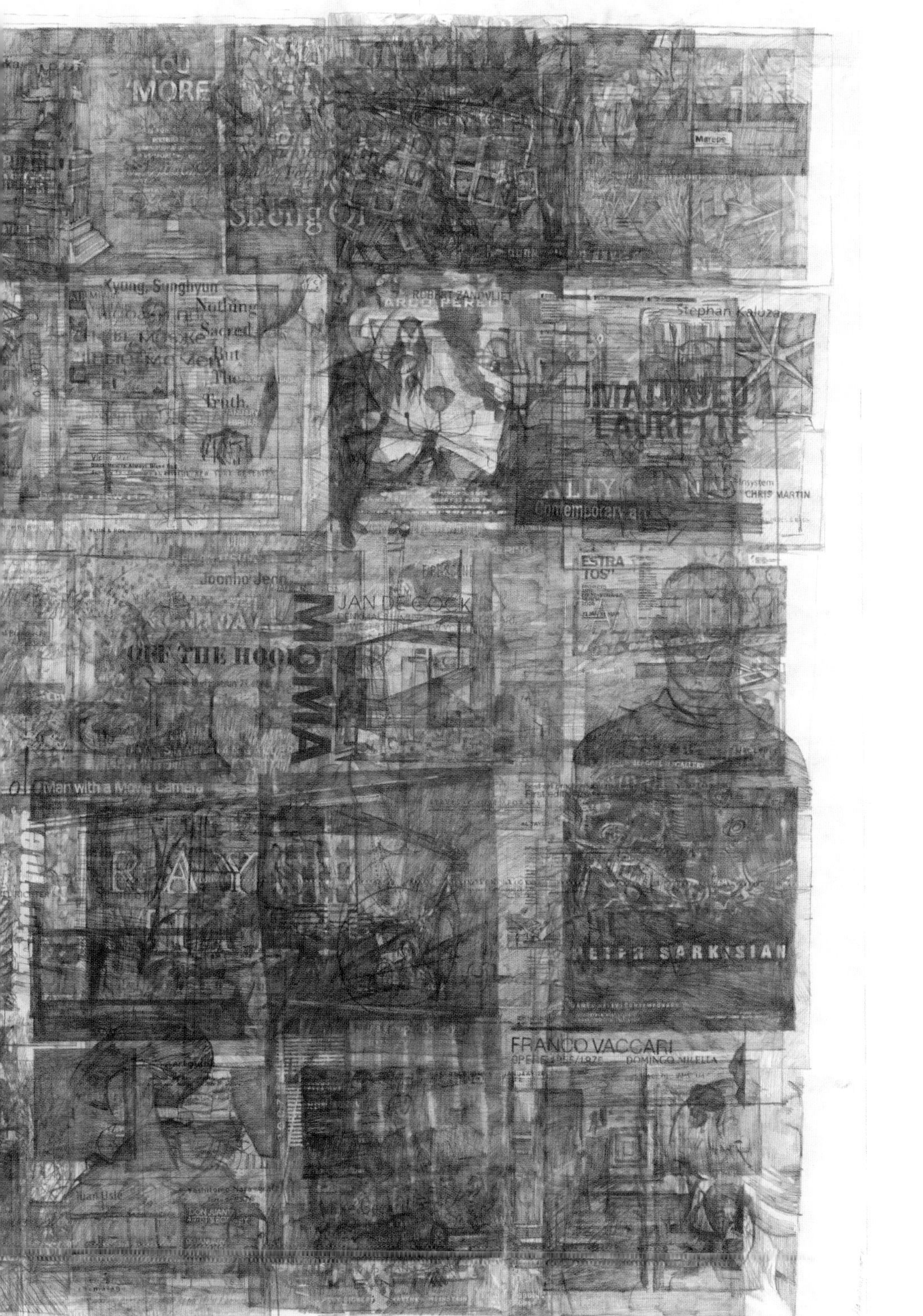

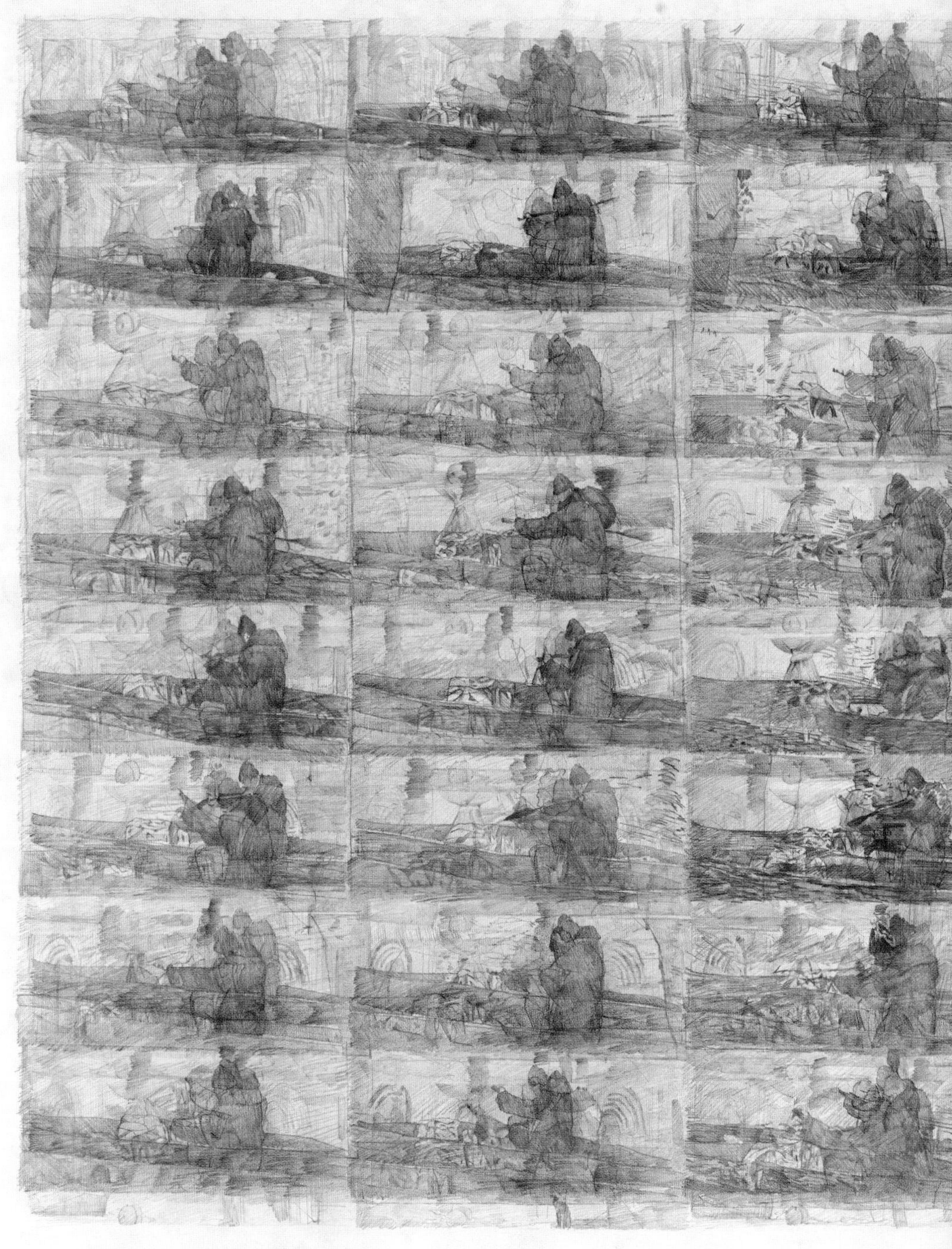